TEN
STEPS
FOR
CHURCH
GROWTH

✦

Donald A. McGavran
and Winfield C. Arn

Published in San Francisco by
HARPER & ROW, PUBLISHERS
New York, Hagerstown, San Francisco, London

Designed by Jim Mennick

Library of Congress Cataloging in Publication Data

McGavran, Donald Anderson
  TEN STEPS FOR CHURCH GROWTH.

  1. Church growth.   I. Arn, Winfield, joint author.
II. Title.
BV652.25.M29 1977   254'.5   76–62950
ISBN 0–06–065351–5
ISBN 0–06–065352–3 pbk.

The text of this book is printed on 100% recycled paper.

78 79 80 81 10 9 8 7 6 5 4 3

TEN
STEPS
FOR
CHURCH
GROWTH

Contents

A Personal Message from the Authors

From Donald A. McGavran:

My initial involvement in Church Growth began with the conviction that God wants people to know Jesus Christ, to become his disciples, to know his power, and to begin living as new creatures. That is a common conviction among Christians, but there is nothing in that conviction itself which would have started the Church Growth school of thought. Along with that, I became acutely conscious that churches were not achieving this goal as effectively as they could.

My conviction grew out of practical experience as the executive secretary-treasurer of our mission in India. I was responsible for administrating extensive operations—seventy missionaries, schools, hospitals, and evangelistic work. The money involved in the operation passed before me. Church growth was minimal considering the energy, people, and dollars invested. Looking beyond our mission, I saw others in the same situation. Many American congregations and denominations were experiencing the same lack of growth.

I asked myself, "Why are we, the church of Jesus Christ, not getting growth commensurate with the mandate, resources, and power God promised?"

The explanation I often heard was "We are doing the best we can. We are working as hard as we can under extremely difficult circumstances." We were working hard, but "difficult circumstances" was not an adequate explanation.

Another common rationalization was "If we were only better Christians, if we only loved the Lord more, prayed more, and forgave each other more, we would grow." I didn't buy that either; my colleagues, Indians and Americans, were good Christians. There were none better! Of course, we had faults, but faults were not the reason for the slight growth of our churches. I still hold the same view: A denomination does not lack growth because of exceeding sinfulness. In most cases, that simply is not true.

Examining the evidence, I came to believe that a major factor in the slow growth of the church was a massive build-up of defensive thinking and rationalizations. Excuses were piled one on top of the other until Christians were surrounded by a wall twenty feet high and thirty feet thick, faced with granite and reinforced with steel bars. Christians were walled off from seeing possibilities and opportunities. They were, unfortunately, comfortable in their courtyard of nongrowth.

Barriers of excuses, rationalizations, and defensive thinking—commonly and falsely based on Scripture—must be destroyed before the church can grow. Recognizing defenses of nongrowth as rationalizations is one contribution of the Church Growth point of view. Twenty years ago it was respectable to parade these "reasons." Today the church at large is beginning to see these "reasons" for what they are—excuses—and they are not offered by serious thinkers.

The next step in pioneering this new way of thinking was *getting the facts*, another significant contribution of the Church Growth school of thought. A few other denominations were experiencing massive growth. The pattern of small growth we knew in our denomination was apparently not necessary.

What happened to me in 1936 is comparable to the reactions of present-day slow-growing U.S. denominations. They are convinced they "cannot grow in the face of contemporary indifference, secularism, and paganism." Then they read about the Southern Baptists, for example, who planted one hundred churches in 1976 in the state of Illinois. The first reaction is anger: "Those Southern Baptists must be planting doubtful Christian churches; if they were good churches, they wouldn't grow." The implications of the statement "doubtful Christian churches grow and good churches don't grow" are devastating. What that statement implies as to the nature of God and the power of Christ should make any denomination ashamed. When the scales fall from its eyes, just as they fell from Saul's, it sees the real situation.

We must get the facts on the growth of congregations and denominations. We must see the many cases of growth that take place. We must see what God is blessing to the growth of his church and what he is not blessing. The history of the church growth movement is partly a history of getting the facts. That is why research is emphasized.

Research simply says, "Let's make many case studies. Let's break through to the real reasons for growth or nongrowth. Let's put diagnostic tools into the hands of pastors, people, missionaries, and evangelists so they will see, clearly and scientifically the real situation." Most of these people are sound Christians. When they see the facts, they will respond in the right way.

As a missionary in India, I was putting in long days, months, and years teaching, preaching, walking and cycling to villages, talking to men and women, employing workers, training workers, building a hospital, attending church and mission committees, baptizing converts. In short, I was working at getting growth in real situations. My life was not at all professorial. I was trying to win village men and women to Christ and organize them into worshiping groups. I was learning the difference between "resistant" people and "mildly resistant" people. If my team of village evangelists and I established one little "church" of four new families out of five two-week long evangelistic campaigns, we felt we were effective. I was working out the "bugs" in the evangelistic machine. I wasn't flying a jet plane. Rather, like the Wright brothers, I was trying to get the plane off the ground. "Church Growth thinking" was on the back burner. Nevertheless, these convictions were gradually forming and hardening during the eighteen years from 1936 to 1954.

I did speak several times to the Landour Community Conference where about two hundred missionaries gather annually. I did speak once in Calcutta to missionaries who worked in what is now Bangladesh, and I spoke to a few other gatherings. Those audiences cordially appreciated what I was speaking about and striving for; otherwise I would never have been invited—I was one missionary among hundreds. But many doubted that growth could be obtained. There was a longing though, a wish that what I was saying would prove true.

When Mrs. McGavran and I came back to the United States on furlough in 1954, our board, the United Christian Missionary Society, kept us home for the next six years. The mission wanted us back, and we were willing to go back, but a combination of circumstances led the board to think we could be more profitably employed at home. They asked me to do a number of Church Growth studies in our various mission fields—Mexico, the Philippines, Thailand, Congo, Jamaica, Puerto Rico, and so on. This work gave me an opportunity to test Church Growth thinking and principles in different situations and to refine these ideas into a global theory, not just an Indian one. This, I believe, was in the providence of God.

At that time (1954–60) I published *Bridges of God* and *How Churches Grow*. I also spoke to meetings of the Division of Overseas Ministries of the National Council of the Churches of Christ, to meetings of the International Missionary Society, and to various denominational gatherings in the United States. As I spoke on Church Growth, I sensed a cordial desire for growth to occur, yet a certain skepticism about whether it could actually happen. My listeners wondered whether what I said about growth was really true. Was concern about church growth legitimate, or was it an undue interest in mere numbers? However you may explain it, nothing came of my addresses in those meetings. I was heard and forgotten.

In 1959 a profound discouragement seized me, and I was on the point of quitting. The leaders of the missions were not hearing what I was saying; they were turning it off. What I had to say had not caught fire. I had done about as much as one person could do, and my efforts seemed futile.

About that time, my wife and I looked at a beautiful little house in the midst of ten acres of walnut trees. We almost bought it and settled in the Aolean Hills, just west of Salem, Oregon. But God had other ideas! Completely beyond any planning of mine, God began to use my convictions. From that time on, starting very small, Church Growth thinking has built up and grown and spread around the world.

In the fifties, European empires in Latfricasia were collapsing; nations were becoming self-governing. Visas were being denied to missionaries. Persecution of the church became not only a possibility but, in many cases, an actuality. A few mission stations were looted and destroyed. Hospitals were burned. European nations were becoming accustomed to the idea that they were no longer ruling the world. Quite naturally, faint hearts asked themselves, "Why are we out here preaching Christ?"

As a result, great pessimism as to the task of the church spread across all nations, east and west. Under that spell, many Christian leaders were rethinking the task of the church. It was no longer "evangelizing the world"; it was "Christians seeking to make the world a better place." Many leaders believed that when Christians had done that they had completely fulfilled their duty. The mission of the church was held neither to involve nor to require world evangelization.

Not everyone was affected by this pessimistic climate. Evangelical, Bible-believing Christians tended to resist it, but leaders of great sections of the church adopted the pessimistic point of view. Missions wallowed in a twenty-year trough, which reached its lowest point around 1968. After that, the facts of history, the acts of God, lessened the flood of pessimism.

A second factor favoring nongrowth in the 1960s was that churches were becoming more and more ecumenical. Through the influence of the ecumenical movement, churches were merging. A cooperative attitude toward other churches is a good thing. We must regard one another with love and friendliness, but it is very easy to slide from that good stance over to "Since practically everyone in this neighborhood is more or less affiliated with some church, there is no need for evangelism. There is no need for converting people. They already have a Baptist, Methodist, Lutheran, or Roman Catholic brand printed on their foreheads. That is all they need."

Such an attitude toward other denominations kept us from seeing that in the United States, huge numbers of people—well over one hundred million at a conservative estimate—were masterless people. They had no consciousness of being disciples of anybody, no awareness of needing a Savior, no obedience to God's will. They were and are living by their own wills and intend to continue—no matter whose "brand" is on their foreheads. Such people are prime prospects for evangelism. They should be won and brought to the Lord. They are prodigals in a far country and need to come back to the Father's house.

These two elements—pessimism concerning missions and an overly optimistic view that everyone is already Christian—prevailed. Other factors also made for slight growth. Religious relativism said, "God has made himself manifest in many different ways, and we should simply move forward, cordially cooperating with people from all religions." Moral relativism said, "Whatever anyone thinks is right, is right for him." These are really stupid ideas; yet they became fairly common, and they mitigated against the growth of the church.

Church Growth thinking arrays itself against all this negative, pessimistic, sub-Christian thought. Part of the twenty-year battle for Church Growth thinking has been to say clearly and firmly as possible that some of these thoughts are wrong. They are not in accord with the will of God. They do not measure up to biblical revelation. They are substantially non-Christian.

As soon as you label these as false beliefs, three-fourths of the church agrees because the heart of the church is still sound. Church Growth thinking has spread so rapidly in the United States in the last few years in part because, as soon as someone says what I have just said, Christians nod their heads and say, "Yes, that is what we believe. That is indeed what the Bible teaches. That is what our church teaches." They come back to the center, to classical biblical thinking.

Church Growth thinking is not narrow. Church Growth thinking is not against cooperative behavior among Christians, nor is it against turning over responsibility to nationals. It is not against social action. It is in favor of these good things. But they must be seen in proportion, and they must not be *substituted* for finding the lost and bringing them to the Father's house.

Proportion is necessary in the local church. Churches are properly engaged in all sorts of good works. For example, keeping up church properties is a good work. I love to see a neat church, beautiful flowers, and a smooth green lawn. I love to hear a well-prepared sermon and a tuneful choir. But these good things must be accompanied by a substantial finding of the lost, bringing them into the Father's house, integrating them in the church, starting new churches, and evangelizing the three billion who have yet to believe. The many good *ministries* of the church must not be substituted for the one *mission* of the church—calling men from death to life.

Several events thrust forward Church Growth thinking. One was establishing the Institute of Church Growth at Northwest Christian College in Eugene, Oregon. Fifty-six students studied there in the first four years—just a handful. The first quarter we had only one student, a veteran missionary from Bolivia. But that first step enabled us to develop courses, assemble reading lists, launch research projects, get book manuscripts under way, establish guidelines, and begin a faculty. One key step was securing Alan Tippett as a research fellow and then an instructor and later as an associate professor of the Institute of Church Growth. Another was holding Church Growth Seminars for missionaries each September at Winona Lake, Indiana.

A second notable event was the publication of the *Church*

Growth Bulletin. Norman Cummings, home director of Overseas Crusades, studied with us in the Institute for Church Growth in 1964. As he was leaving, he said, "What you are saying here should be heard everywhere."

I responded, "I know, but we have neither funds nor publication know-how."

He said, "Let us pay for printing and mailing the *Church Growth Bulletin*. We will keep the subscription list and do all the business. You just provide the manuscript." Overseas Crusades has been doing that ever since—a wonderful service to the cause of Christ. As a result, Church Growth thinking has spread through the whole world.

The third step was moving to Fuller Theological Seminary and becoming a full-fledged graduate school. I recruited a splendid faculty of five able teachers; all had been missionaries. That enabled us to promote Church Growth on a broad and effective front.

A fourth important happening was beginning the William Carey Library, really a publishing house producing books about the Great Commission Missions. There is an extensive market for missionary books, and one publishing company cannot possibly saturate it. However, the William Carey Library, plus the *Church Growth Bulletin*, does penetrate many areas of the world.

A fifth notable event, and one which developed Church Growth in America, was founding the Institute for American Church Growth and Fuller Evangelistic Association's Department of Church Growth. Through these agencies we began to conduct seminars, workshops, and pastors' conferences dealing with Church Growth in almost every state in the Union.

Sound and color films dramatizing Church Growth were made available to churches. New books were written about Church Growth in the United States. The Southern Baptists provided many examples for the rest of the church. Hundreds of Church Growth seminars and workshops, a dozen regional *Church Growth Bulletins* in various languages, and Church Growth centers helped spread a more biblical way of thinking about the duty and privilege of the church.

Presently, Church Growth is coming into its own. Bands of men and women in many countries have now come to share in Church Growth thinking. They are seeing that a great deal more growth can be obtained, that salvation can spread wider and freer, and that the river of life can flow faster. Able ministers of the gospel, missionaries, and national leaders (white, brown, yellow, black, speaking many different tongues) are adding different emphases to fit many different situations, and they are seeing their parts of God's church grow.

Today there is unprecedented receptivity to the message of Christ. Today people are more winnable; the nations, the tribes, and the castes of the world are more responsive to the gospel than they have ever been before. There is no need to believe that pessimism and indifference outweigh God's grace. The Church Growth point of view is becoming known, believed, expressed, and explored. The church and mankind will reap great benefits as a result.

There is, of course, the danger that Church Growth would become a fad. I have seen fads in churches and missions sweep across the United States and around the world. I have wondered if Church Growth is going to become a fad, but I don't think so for two reasons.

First, it is very close to the unswerving purpose of God. That will assure it is being carried on. Second, an extraordinary number of people are dedicating their lives to church growth—which is simply biblical missions. These individuals will carry Christ's mission forward. It will take different shapes but will be sound at the center. It will demonstrate, incorporate, and incarnate the various emphases we have been talking about. Churches in Latin America, Africa, and Asia are awakening to evangelism. Quite frankly, they haven't been evangelistic enough. They were just like churches in North America. The devil was defeating them just like he was defeating us, but today they are rousing to evangelistic opportunities and duties. I see them establishing missionary societies and sending out missionaries to the unevangelized portions of the world. I see them welcoming missionaries from Europe and America.

All of this causes me to believe that in the next twenty-five years, or maybe in the next fifty years, we will see an unprecedented advance of the church. I pray to God this may happen.

From Winfield C. Arn:

I came to Church Growth from a background in evangelism. As the director of a large evangelistic organization aimed primarily at winning youth, we had what we thought was an effective approach to a very winnable segment of society. A distinctive of this ministry was a youth rally where attendance of over two thousand per meeting was common. This rally included a variety of activities to attract youth and concluded with a message on salvation and an invitation to make a decision for Christ. Week after week, with few exceptions, five to fifty young people would respond and make a "decision." This appeared, at the time, to be very effective evangelism. Those who made "decisions" were counseled, sent literature, and encouraged to attend a church. We kept in touch with them and followed their spiritual progress as much as possible.

While much good was accomplished in this ministry, I sensed problems. What happened to those who made "decisions"? Did they become growing, reproducing Christians? Did they become actively involved in a church? Some did, of course, and those individuals became the public illustrations used to validate this method of evangelism. But what of the others? What were the long-term results? What were the actual facts? I determined to find the answer.

I researched, collected data, interviewed, and analyzed until I had a body of significant facts. The results were startling! The fruit which remained was seriously lacking! The evangelistic effort included prayer, a fine staff, and proclamation of the gospel; yet much fruit seemed to fall to the ground, decay, and die.

At this same time, I served as leader for an area-wide evangelistic crusade which brought to Portland, Oregon, a leading evangelist. He was accompanied by a highly organized and efficient staff for a two-week evangelistic campaign. Hundreds of prayer groups were formed. Billboards covered the city. Daily newspaper ads and television commercials foretold the event. Counselors were trained. Finances were raised. The crusade was held, decisions were made, and all acclaimed it a success.

When it was all over and the team had gone, I again researched the fruit. To my dismay, it was seriously lacking. What was wrong?

Friends gave me different counsel. "Don't worry," said one, "if just one soul was saved, it was worth it all." That didn't satisfy me. Another reassured me, "God keeps the records. Our job is to preach the gospel." I couldn't fully accept that either. A third person said, "Some seed falls on good ground; some falls on bad ground. You take what you get." But that wasn't enough truth for me. There had to be a better answer.

The problem, I soon discovered, extended beyond evangelistic crusades. The disease affected the church itself. The home missions secretary of a large denomination described it: "There is what we must describe as an 'obedience gap.' Statistics show a mortality rate of 75 percent among new converts. Why is it that only one convert in four ever makes it to the point of church membership?"

Struggling with the problem of "the fruit which remains," I began to find answers. For example, I discovered that evangelistic efforts can be well advertised, financed, promoted, prayed for, and evoke decisions, yet be relatively fruitless if they are not a vital part of the local church ministry. In fact, the closer evangelism is integrated into a local church, the greater will be the "fruit that remains."

A second discovery was the need to change the goal from *decisions* to *disciples*. What a difference this made! A *decision* suggests a moment of time, a solo event. A *disciple* suggests a way of life, incorporation into the Body. The concept of *decision* has outlived its usefulness. The word is unbiblical and inadequate to describe the life commitment called for in Scripture.

A third discovery was that evangelism is more effective, not as a special once-a-year emphasis, but when built into the fabric of the church. When evangelism is an integral part of the continued program of every church, when Christians are meaningfully involved in outreach, two things will happen: (1) Those involved will grow and mature as they learn to witness, study the Word, and learn to pray. And their numbers will grow! (2) There will be more "fruit which remains." When a new convert has found Christ through the efforts of members of a local congregation, relationships have been established. A natural follow-up solves the problem that plagues most professional evangelistic efforts— the "follow-up gap." The closer the sociological, psychological, relational bond between new converts and established Christians in a local church, the greater the yield of fruit.

My pilgrimage to Church Growth really started in frustration and dissatisfaction with evangelistic methods I had seen and been a part of in America. My search led me to the local church. The church is God's plan for making disciples and for winning a world.

I determined to bring any expertise I had into focus at that point. To acquire more expertise in Church Growth thinking, I visited the School of World Mission and Church Growth at Fuller Theological Seminary. When I inquired concerning resources and materials for American Church Growth, I found that Dr. Donald McGavran and C. Peter Wagner were team-teaching a course applying world principles of Church Growth to the American scene. I immediately became a part of that group. As I listened and learned, I realized here was the effective approach to evangelism for which I had been searching. In those hours, I experienced my third birth—"conversion" to Church Growth thinking.

As an American churchman, I saw the necessity of applying Church Growth concepts and insights to this nation. After my growth "conversion," I began to apply gifts and abilities God had given to help bring Church Growth thinking to America. The first step was *How to Grow a Church*. This book is being used to introduce church growth concepts to America. Next came films: *How to Grow a Church, Reach Out and Grow, And They Said It Couldn't Be Done!, Planned Parenthood for Churches* (see appendix for description and source). Articles have been written, seminars have been held, curricula developed, and God is using Church Growth thinking to increase his church.

The Institute for American Church Growth began in a "leap of faith." I resigned a comfortable denominational position and, without any visible means of support or even the assurance that America would receive Church Growth thinking, I "climbed the trapeze" about which you read in the last chapter. My strength was the knowledge that God wanted his church to grow in America. That was enough! The institute was organized to accomplish that end. Since then, God has used this ministry to enable individual churches, groups of churches, and denominations to see new possibilities and to grow!

The Institute has four purposes:

1. To motivate and encourage evangelism and church growth in America.
2. To enable individual churches to devise strategy and bold plans for growth.
3. To help pastors and lay people understand their growth problems and apply reproducible principles of growth.
4. To serve as a resource for the church at large in its growth efforts.

These purposes are implemented through: (1) conducting seminars, workshops, and training sessions; (2) carrying on a program of research and development; (3) communicating through a variety of methods and media to enable churches to reach their fullest potential in growth and outreach; (4) providing a service of diagnosis, research, and consultation to churches.

Church Growth thinking is having a considerable impact on churches. A few years ago, few people had heard the term *Church Growth*. Today it's becoming part of the vocabulary of the American church. Hundreds and hundreds of churches can now give testimony that Church Growth thinking brings growth. Within a very few years Church Growth will be a priority item, if it is not already, for every major denomination. The change has occurred for several reasons. First, the significant decline many congregations and major denominations have suffered. Second, actually seeing millions of people across America who are undiscipled and unchurched, and realizing there is a rich harvest field all around us. Third, a return to a solid, biblical position and the conviction that God wants lost people found. Fourth, the growth results some churches are experiencing has awakened others to the possibilities.

Today there is an exciting new ferment. God is doing a new thing in and through his church. The principles and concepts of Church Growth are being used for effective evangelism in America and around the world. God has called the Institute to minister by helping churches and denominations grow. Using diagnostic tools and applying reproducible principles of Church Growth, the Institute has seen the Lord pour out his blessing to the increase of his church. Supports and illustrations from individual churches, consortia of churches, conferences, districts, presbyteries, synods, dioceses, and entire denominations unquestionably affirm that Church Growth thinking, when properly applied, brings growth. The goal of the institute is to enable churches to become all they are capable of being, growing to their full stature, fulfilling their function in God's plan and purpose.

1

The First Step:
Discovering Church Growth
Principles

Join us in discovering Church Growth principles step by step. We will explore ten dynamic growth principles, but the list is far from exhaustive. You, as a "co-researcher," will be formulating principles of your own, for new Church Growth principles are continually being discovered. They are not developed with a "made in USA" label but are world-wide in scope. Principles of Church Growth can be discovered by anyone willing to see through "Church Growth eyes," not only by professionals. In fact, many co-researchers are making exciting discoveries right now.

What are Church Growth principles? How are they discovered?

A Church Growth principle is a universal truth which, when properly interpreted and applied, contributes significantly to the growth of churches and denominations. It is a truth of God which leads his church to spread his Good News, plant church after church, and increase his Body.

Discovering Church Growth principles is not difficult. One observes where the church is growing, where God is blessing the efforts of his servants with factual, actual church growth, where the number of members is increasing and new congregations are being born, and where men and women are introduced to Jesus Christ, commit their lives to him, and become responsible members of his church.

When one sees that happening, he or she asks why. One observes and studies the various factors, efforts, prayers, witness, passion, teaching, education, biblical base, and outreach from which this growth emerges. Carefully analyzed and truthfully described findings lead to one or more Church Growth principles.

In discovering Church Growth principles it is important to find *real* reasons. Often superficial explanations obscure basic principles. A good researcher digs to bedrock. Many reasons for church growth are alleged. They represent an erroneous judgment or, more frequently, a partial judgment. They take one cause for church growth and state it as if it were the *only* cause.

Consequently, there is considerable need for skill in thinking scientifically about the growth of the church. A researcher must weigh the various factors. Although factors one and two play a small part, and factors three and four play a more significant part, the really crucial factor may be number five. Studying a book like this and *How to Grow a Church*, along with other Church Growth books,* helps pastors, laymen, and students become skilled in thinking accurately and scientifically about the growth of the church.

The church viewed scientifically? Aren't you ruling out the spiritual? How can you apply scientific principles to the spiritual realm?

Viewing the church scientifically, yet reverently, is not unspiritual. The Lord said, "You observe the trees, and when they bud, you say, 'Summer is near'" (see Matt. 24:32). We are to use the same process in thinking about spiritual matters. The Lord has

---

*The basic book is Donald A. McGavran, *Understanding Church Growth* (Grand Rapids: Eerdmans, 1970).

given us minds and expects us to use them. "You shall love the Lord your God with all your . . . *mind*" (Matt. 22:37, RSV, italics mine).

The scientific method is thinking about things of the kingdom with the same astute observation, common sense, and good judgment that we use in thinking about other areas of life. The scientist works with specific tools; so does the Church Growth researcher. For example, the statistical approach is a way of discovering truth, and it is effective in studying churches and collecting data. One co-researcher recently found that if the number of members being added to the church were a certain proportion of the total membership, the church was growing. If the number being added fell below that proportion, the church was declining. This finding, if it proves true in other denominations and circumstances, will add an accurate way to estimate future growth or decline of a church or denomination.

You are invited to share in the exciting discovery of growth principles, to secure research data where you live, and to come alive to a new way of thinking—Church Growth thinking! In this book we are not saying, "Here are the conclusions. These are all you have to learn." We are saying, "Journey with us. Begin thinking about your church in new ways. Discover new ways of thinking about your church and community, develop Church Growth eyes that see more accurately the various parts, the homogeneous units, the responsive segments of the community which can be won." Church Growth eyes see the priorities needed for growth. This is the kind of thinking you are invited to share.

Some of you co-researchers will not be Americans. You know, of course, that Church Growth principles are world-wide in their implications and applications. Growth principles discovered anywhere are of value everywhere.

Mankind is a remarkable unity. People everywhere cry when they hurt, laugh when they're happy, become angry when insulted. People think and act very much alike. Consequently, the way people anywhere receive Jesus Christ and become responsible members of his church has great meaning for the church everywhere. There are, of course, cultural and linguistic differences; Church Growth principles are generally applicable world-wide because of the common denominator—people. For example, the concept of reaching families as families applies world-wide. In a tightly woven tribe, reaching families might result in a "people movement"; in the United States, where there are no tightly woven tribes, it would result in the addition of strong families. Since family affection is found everywhere, the basic principle that families like to do things together influences growth in the United States and abroad.

Church Growth principles hurdle cultural and geographic barriers. What applies in New England applies in Wisconsin. There are differences, but these are relatively minor. Any intelligent person can screen out the things applicable in one location only and use the things that are applicable everywhere.

Today the world is a "global village." It is one unit, and Church Growth principles have significant value for world-wide evangelization. There are, of course, cultural-geographical barriers, but the commonalties of all men are many, and the unity of mankind is a fact. Hence, *people* become the focus for Church Growth thinking.

Am I needed in this world-wide effort?

Yes! You and many like you! Co-researchers and research in many areas are needed. There are two kinds of researchers: (1) The academician who goes off to graduate school for a few years and does an extensive piece of investigation which he tenders for a degree; (2) Practicing pastors and lay people who occupy positions of responsibility in the church. The second is possibly more important.

For example, a layman interviewed men and women who had recently become converts to Christianity "from the world" (people whose parents were not Christians). He spent hours with each one until he came to an accurate opinion as to the real reasons, under those particular circumstances, each had become Christian.

The results of his research were helpful in reaching other people for Christ.

The doors are wide open for lay people and pastors to study their own churches, denominations, and communities. As this is done, within a few years we shall begin to know a great deal more about the processes through which God has blessed his church with growth. The end result will be a new outpouring of God's grace and power in the world through his church!

Today we stand on the edge of the greatest expansion of the church the world has ever seen. To those reared on large doses of pessimism, hearing every Sunday about the post-Christian era or the indifference of people to Christ, this stance may seem unduly optimistic. Yet the facts clearly indicate that the church is expanding greatly and will continue to do so.

God is not going to be defeated! Jesus Christ is not powerless! The arm of the Lord is not weak! God is the Father Almighty. The church of Jesus Christ has abundant resources and excellencies. It is now evidencing strengths and goodness and kindness such as no other organization even dreams about.

As we begin developing Church Growth eyes and see the possibilities, as we discover methods that prove effective and discard methods that are clearly ineffective, we will find ourselves in a new age. With God's blessing and the indwelling of the Holy Spirit, we shall see the church advancing in many areas of the world.

Even today, all Africa south of the Sahara is in the process of becoming substantially Christian. There is a mighty Christian movement in Korea. In Indonesia one hundred thousand Muslims—for the first time in one thousand years—have recently become Christians. These are good signs. If such advance for Christ can happen in Africa, Korea, and Indonesia, it can happen elsewhere. A great vitality is evident in church planting: Outside North America one thousand new churches open their doors for the first time every Sunday! Five thousand new churches are planted each year in Latin America alone. In world overview, one sees a forward surge in Christian vigor and liberation that many

Christians find hard to believe. Current projections are that within twenty-five years most of the world's Christians will be found in what used to be called mission lands.

In America also, church after church is coming alive and reaching out in new and dynamic ways. The Spirit of God seems to be breathing into his church new energy for outreach, evangelism, and growth. Multitudes of people in America today are receptive to the gospel. Churches that recognize this truth and act upon it are growing. The Lord is giving the increase!

Multitudes of winnable people are waiting to be won. Of the approximately 214,000,000 Americans, 150,000,000 are either pagans or marginal Christians who not only *need* to be but *can* be discipled. Some of these winnable people live around every church. The common impression held by many Christians, that the people in their church's ministry area are so indifferent they cannot be won, is not really true. Such negativism reflects the state of mind of these Christians more than it does the reality around them.

Can my church grow?

The Church Growth principles enumerated and illustrated in this book will facilitate growth. They will help local congregations. You see, the church has two ministries: Caring for those already in the church and reaching out to the lost. It's helpful to think of these as ministry *to* the Body and ministry *through* the Body. We must recognize that churches have a built-in tendency to be self-centered and ingrown. They focus most of their energies and dollars inward. "Tending the store" must give way to vigorous outreach. It is necessary that we begin to see unreached people and then pray, plan, and program to win them. Unless we reach out to those unreached and find ways to bring them in, there won't be significant growth.

To accomplish this task, we must start thinking in new ways about our congregation. We must discern the various homogeneous parts of the Body. We must also begin seeing the community in new ways. A community is a tremendously complex mosaic. Each facet has needs, interests, likes, and dislikes. As we discover these different pieces and direct evangelistic, witnessing, and service efforts toward them, we will find responsiveness. As lay people discover Church Growth principles and incorporate them into the warp and woof of the congregation, new possibilities of growth will appear. These principles will be of inestimable value in helping local churches grow and accomplish their purpose. Let each church become all that God intended, growing to its full stature and fulfilling its part in the larger Body of Christ.

Why is growth so important?

Church Growth is directly related to God's will. God wants his church to grow. The Lord Jesus, on the occasion of his last appearance to the apostles, said, "All authority in heaven and on earth has been given to me. Go therefore and make disciples" (Matt. 28:18, 19, RSV). It's just as plain as that. Any church not concerned with growth and discipleship is really disobeying God and is doing what is *not* pleasing to him. His express will is that the good news of the gospel be communicated to all people, all classes, all races, and all languages near and far, geographically and culturally.

The goal is that there be a living church of Jesus Christ in every segment of society on earth. Every segment of American society, or any society, should be throbbing with Christian life, full of groups of committed Christians, loving, serving, praying, growing in the Word, reaching out! Each local church has a part in fulfilling the Great Commission!

The "church" in the United States and in the world is made up of local churches. There are also unions, associations, presbyteries, dioceses, synods, and denominations. As specific congregations and the larger administration units obey the Great Commission more intelligently, more effectively, and more fervently, the church will grow. As Christians refine their methods, develop Church Growth eyes, feel church growth responsibility, communicate the gospel, and educate those who are won until they become responsible Christians, the church as a whole will receive the abundant blessing God wants to give.

But that isn't the kind of experience we are having at our church.

We hear many reasons why churches do not grow. Actually, many of the reasons people give for nongrowth are nothing more than rationalizations built on decades of stagnation. They are the debris of defeat. People grow accustomed to believing that nongrowth is normal.

Some Christians not only voice excuses but actually seem to believe that God wants his church to remain small and weak. This is clearly contrary to Scripture. God wants his church to grow! God wants people to know the Savior. God says "whosoever will." Scripture lays great emphasis upon the height, depth, and breadth of God's love. Anybody, everybody, ought to have the privilege of hearing the Good News, making an intelligent response, and becoming a disciple and responsible member of the Body.

Behind the Church Growth movement, is the pulsating belief that multitudes of people are winnable. Not everyone, of course. Many will reject the Savior, but large numbers are winnable. Church Growth principles are powerful tools, effective as we work together to fulfill the Great Commission.

QUESTIONS FOR REVIEW AND DISCUSSION

1. What is the difference between a Church Growth principle and a Church Growth method? Illustrate.
2. What steps would you take in discovering Church Growth principles for your church?
3. How would you go about applying the scientific method, as discussed in this chapter, to your church?

4. What does the Great Commission goal mean for your church? How is it being implemented?
5. What steps might be taken to enable members in the church see more clearly the goal of the Great Commission and its implementation for your fellowship?
6. What concepts and references in the New and Old Testaments support the contention that "God wants his church to grow"?

2

Churches Grow As They Respect Biblical Principles

The Church Growth point of view is thoroughly biblical. A Church Growth person respects biblical principles—truths revealed in Scripture, found throughout revelation, and believed as foundational to the faith.

The relationships between biblical principles and Church Growth tie Church Growth thinking firmly to the Bible. Church Growth is the will of God. It has nothing to do with self-aggrandizement. Growth is God's business, carried out at God's command. The following seven biblical principles do not comprise an exhaustive doctrinal statement; they do suggest a way to begin Church Growth thinking and to see through Church Growth eyes.

I. RESPECTING BIBLICAL PRINCIPLES MEANS ACCEPTING THE BIBLE AS FINAL AUTHORITY.

Scripture is the major source for Church Growth thinking. The New Testament is a series of Church Growth documents. The Gospels, the Book of Acts, and the Epistles were written by missionaries for missionaries. They were written by Church Growth people to Church Growth people to help the church grow.

When the Scriptures are read in this light, they are really understood. When a static church reads the New Testament, it misses many important truths; but as the Scripture is read through Church Growth eyes, one discovers that it bubbles with Church Growth information, illustrations, principles, and priorities.

Some people, unfortunately, endeavor to explain away the Bible. Origen, an early Church Father, explained Scripture away allegorically. Today, some would explain it away anthropologically. They say, "In those circumstances, in that culture, the Bible meant that; but that is not true for us today." While it is true that the Bible was spoken to that culture and to those people in those circumstances, it was given for *our* edification. It was not spoken to that culture *only*. God revealed his truth for that culture and for all times and all men.

For example, the Bible clearly states that we are to "forgive our enemies." The cultural interpretation of that statement would be, "The Lord was speaking to the people of Palestine. We must see behind the words to what the Lord meant. He was speaking to a weak, subjected people. He was saying 'Deal realistically with your enemies. You had better forgive them because they are powerful. If you don't forgive them, they will destroy you.' Had he been speaking to a dominant ruling nation, he would have said something different: 'Destroy your enemies. That's the way to deal with them!'" The Bible must not be explained away.

At the Nairobi meeting of the World Council of Churches, the United Bible Societies presented a new way of looking at the parable of the prodigal son. The principle of translation, known as dynamic equivalents, was applied, not only to specific cultural metaphors such as "fell on his neck and kissed him," but also the basic teaching of the parable. The presentation suggested that the younger son was right to break with the father in the interests of being himself and that the older son was right to stand up to his father and that the parable is really an openended story to show how the father can keep both sons. While this interpretation speaks to the problems and tensions in individualistic Western family life, it can by no stretch of the imagination be considered a valid exegesis of the biblical passage. It explains away the Bible. While it may gain a little by "modernizing" the application, it loses almost everything by a loose, low view of the authority of the Scriptures. The first biblical principle Church Growth men emphasize is faithfulness to the plain meaning of the Bible, our authority.

The infallibility and authority of Scripture, however, must not be interpreted to mean that it is unnecessary to understand the context in which the words were spoken. Understanding what the words meant to those who first heard them is essential. It is also essential to see the thrust of the *whole* Bible. Furthermore, new ideas are continually breaking forth from the pages of the Bible. More light, truth, and power are always emerging from the eternal Scriptures. This new light is always in harmony with the light already revealed. The Bible does not contradict itself.

Does Church Growth thinking go beyond biblical principles, using methods or ideas not found in Scripture?

We live in a day of a marvelous explosion of knowledge. This is in the providence of God; he intended it. God has given to man, particularly in the last few centuries, an amazing amount of knowledge about our world. He expects us to apply this knowledge in line with biblical principles. When we use this knowledge —geography, anthropology, sociology, psychology, and many other areas—in line with biblical principles, we are doubly right. We are using the tools God has given us, and we are using them for ends that he blesses.

2. RESPECTING BIBLICAL PRINCIPLES SEES PEOPLE OUTSIDE CHRIST AS LOST.

This is the basic reason Christians press forward with the growth and multiplication of churches. We remind ourselves constantly that people without Jesus Christ are *really lost*. This is the solid witness of Scripture, and it is amply supported from history, life, and experience. The only way people can come to the Father

is by Jesus Christ. Every Christian needs to focus on this truth
from Scripture. Respecting biblical principles means being convinced from Scripture that men are really lost unless they believe
on Jesus.

Intellectually, most Christians and most churches believe that
those outside Christ are lost, but does that truth get into every
practical aspect of thinking, planning, and programming? Many
church members tend to see Saviorless and Masterless neighbors
and friends as not lost, not condemned, not bound for a Christless
eternity. But Christians who form their opinions in opposition to
the scriptural view are mistaken; they need a biblical conviction of
mankind's lostness.

Recognizing this basic principle means that we must take seriously both the lost in general and the lost in our own ministry
area. We must not believe we have already won all the lost who
can be found. This produces a comfortable feeling and creates a
"fog" through which those who are lost cannot be clearly seen.

Sometimes the fog causes Christians to say that the lost are
indifferent and so sinful they cannot possibly be saved; sometimes
the fog causes Christians to say that they themselves need to "get
better" before those who are lost will listen. Both these excuses
are rationalizations; God wants lost people found. Found people
are the precious stones God uses to build his church.

3. RESPECTING BIBLICAL PRINCIPLES MEANS AFFIRMING THAT GOD'S LOVE AND CONCERN IS FOR ALL PEOPLE.

Christians need to be certain that their affections are not nar-
rowly limited to one small part of mankind but extend to all men
and women. As members of the Body, we are co-workers with
God in fulfilling his unswerving purpose to redeem men. God
does not want any to perish. Scripture is clear on that! He wishes
all men to be saved. God's desire must be our desire. While some
will reject his invitation, our heavenly Father wants all to be saved.

His concern is for the salvation of multitudes—hundreds of
thousands of different ethnic and language units, social structures,
geographic locations, and economic entities, all of which will

some day form a bewildering variety of churches. God loves them all; he is the God of all.

The United States is not one monolithic population. It is a marvelous mosaic made up of thousands of pieces . . .all kinds of peoples, a pluralistic society. Understanding the various pieces of this mosaic helps us see God's overarching concern. Often we are blind to other cultures, including those in our own country; yet discovering God's unwavering concern for *all* cures our blindness and extends our vision.

Christians who form convictions on the sure rock of biblical principles are just as concerned with men and women in other cultures as with those in their own. They realize that Caucasians are no more precious in the Lord's sight than Chinese, Japanese, Chicanos, Arabs, Blacks, and Amerindians. According to the Bible, we are all God's children, equally precious. God is no respecter of persons. The Lord Jesus died for all.

4. RESPECTING BIBLICAL PRINCIPLES MEANS BELIEVING THAT CHRIST IS THE ONLY WAY.

The Good News is that God has provided *one way*, a beautiful way, the way of his Son, the way of the cross, the way through the tomb to joyful resurrection. This one way is "whoever believes on the Son will have everlasting life." This is the gospel. Men and women cannot earn salvation by good deeds. Salvation comes by believing on the Savior. Believers are justified *by faith*. When they receive Jesus Christ as their Lord and Savior, their sins are really forgiven. This is foundational.

No man-made religion offers a way of salvation, forgiveness of sins, peace with God, reconciliation with the Father, and the indwelling presence of the Holy Spirit. Christianity is unique.

5. RESPECTING BIBLICAL PRINCIPLES MEANS OBEDIENCE TO THE LEADING OF THE HOLY SPIRIT.

The Holy Spirit commands; it is up to us to obey! The Christian's response is "Speak, Lord, for your servant hears" (see 1

Sam. 3:9). Such obedience is a major factor in the growth of any church.

Involved in this obedience is the conscious desire for the Spirit's direction. When confronted with problems and uncertainties, the Christian seeks God's direction. A congregation or a Church Growth person faced with a problem prays, "Father, I've endeavored to gather all the facts available, and still I'm uncertain which is the best decision. I need your guidance and direction. I'm asking for your leading. I am listening for your instructions." Following such a prayer, action can be taken by faith in the confident assurance that the Holy Spirit will indeed lead.

The leading and power of the Holy Spirit is illustrated in page after page of the New Testament. The Acts of the Apostles could be accurately called the "Acts of the Holy Spirit," for the Holy Spirit, acting in and through the church, enabled these Christians to turn their "world upside down" (Acts 17:6).

Early Christians were filled with the Spirit and empowered by the Spirit. In the Spirit's strength and power, Barnabas, Stephen, Paul, and other leaders, along with ordinary Christians, did what was, humanly speaking, impossible. Through history, ordinary men and women, empowered by the Holy Spirit, did extraordinary things.

The same Holy Spirit who walked across the pages of the New Testament in glorious acts is present today. He will and does empower Christians when they try to do God's will. He will and does empower churches when they intend obediently to carry out the Father's will. Remember, God wills the growth of his church, and the Holy Spirit gives power for such growth.

6. RESPECTING BIBLICAL PRINCIPLES MEANS PRAYING INTELLIGENTLY AND SPECIFICALLY FOR THE GROWTH OF THE CHURCH.

Have you ever heard anyone in a prayer meeting pray specifically for the *growth* of the church? Perhaps you have, but unfortunately, many prayer meetings sound more like infirmary roll calls. Infirmities of the body often take precedence over infirmities of the soul. We should of course pray for the sick, for those who need physical healing, but should we not be more concerned for "the sick" who need forgiveness of sin and spiritual healing?

Churches have been holding prayer meetings for years, but in many cases they haven't seen growth because Christians seldom petition God for growth. They don't pray specifically for the conversion of close friends and loved ones. They don't pray for families by name. They don't pray that new churches might be planted. They don't pray specifically for the discipling of others. In other words, they don't pray intelligently for growth.

What a transforming change might occur if, in church after church across America, sustained, passionate praying for growth might be part of every meeting, until such praying penetrated every Christian's conscience. God will hear and answer. Unprecedented growth of a magnitude hitherto unknown would take place.

God's blessing is being seen in Korea where in predawn prayer meetings thousands gather to seek God's face. With such committed praying, is it any wonder that a great surge of spiritual power is at work across that nation? Is it any wonder that people are being discipled and that churches are multiplying? The same principle applies in every country and every church.

7. RESPECTING BIBLICAL PRINCIPLES MEANS SEEING THE CHURCH AS THE BODY OF CHRIST.

The Church Growth perspective takes a high view of the church. The church is absolutely essential. It is not just one organization among many through which God works. It is *the* Body of Christ, not just *a* Body of Christ. It is not just *a* Bride of Christ, but *the* Bride of Christ.

Respecting biblical principles means that we hold the church to be a necessary part of God's plan for the salvation and discipling of men and nations. They must not only believe in Jesus Christ but must become responsible members of his church. The Bible requires that. If we take the Bible seriously, we cannot hold any other viewpoint.

Becoming a Christian means becoming part of the Body, part of the family of God, part of the household of faith. The saved become part of the redeemed community. They live in the community, mutually supporting, encouraging, and helping others in the Body. Believers must become part of the church; otherwise the reality of their belief is in question. This high view of the church must be maintained. A low view of the church, held by secular relativists, is that belonging to the church is more or less a matter of choice. If you like it, you belong; if you don't, you don't. Church Growth Christians reject any such low view.

Hasn't the church often failed?

Yes, the church has failed. Perhaps it will fail again, but the glorious thing is that despite these failures the Lord still indwells it. The Lord takes his church, when its faith grows dim, and turns it around, just as he did the men on the road to Emmaus. They didn't believe. They were downcast and pessimistic about the future. Then the Lord appeared to them, and their hearts burned anew. They turned right around and became new people. When Jesus said, "I will build my church," he meant it. When the church gets out of line, his guiding hand brings it back.

It is definitely the purpose of God that his church become the instrument of salvation and discipling for the entire world. We must live in the light of that hope. We must be optimistic, not foolishly, unthinkingly optimistic, but realistically assessing the difficulties and, more importantly, the opportunities.

Let the church be all that it was created capable of becoming. This calls for reproduction, part of the Church's basic function. A sound body is reproductive; reproduction is a normal God-given function of the human body. Reproduction of the church is also a God-given urge, and the church should not suppress it.

Unfortunately, many denominations have forgotten this. Some deny the urge. They determine to remain sterile, non-productive parts of the Body. Their mental attitudes prevent them from bearing daughter churches.

Yet, God can heal them. As their Church Growth eyes develop, they see new needs and opportunities. When they study receptive and resistant units, the winnable and **unwinnable**, they discover where churches can be born and grow.

But we are expected to do so many things.

God expects his church to do many good things, but these must be arranged in order of priorities. The church needs to see its various options and then order its priorities. Any church sensitive to the leading of the Holy Spirit, taking the authority of the Bible seriously, praying intelligently and systematically about its mission, will be able to arrange its priorities in a way which will please God.

The church serves in many different ways; however, it must never forget its primary and irreplaceable task—bringing lost children back to the Father's house. Winning the lost is a fundamental function through which the church is re-created. The church, both as individuals and as orgainzations, is continually dying. Unless it is re-created by winning the lost, it fails in its greatest service to mankind, and soon there will be no church.

Christians often mistakenly assume that their church is always going to be there. They have a beautiful building and wonderful Christian brothers and sisters. Of course, their church is always going to be there! But the church is always just one generation away from extinction. Unless there is continual reproduction, there isn't going to be any church. Evangelism is a top priority. God uses it to create the church. When the church is created, it does God's work in the world.

Is building the church man's work or God's?

In answering that question, keep two concepts before you. First, God is immensely concerned that lost men be saved. He sent his Son to live and die that the lost be found and restored to communion with God. Second, our Lord left the carrying out of his program entirely to twelve men, and then to the church. We must *act* as though we alone were responsible and *pray* as though God alone were responsible.

Paul's words are helpful. He wrote to the Corinthian church, "I . . . planted, Apollos watered; but God gave the increase" (1 Cor. 3:6). When a church grows, God has given the increase. Yet man has planted, watered, and nurtured. God has given these tasks into men's hands; they are man's responsibility.

There is a beautiful combination of God and man in the growth of his church. Churches intensely conscious of God's presence and God's passion for the salvation of men find they have all kinds of unsuspected resources in themselves. Conversely, churches in which the vision of God's concern for the lost world grows dim gradually wither and die.

A good theology of the church should be fulfilled in day-to-day personal experience. In worship, in committee meetings, and in home and business life Christians should think of their congregations in dynamic, not static, terms. We must see not only a church building on the corner but a church whose people are obedient to Christ in their daily lives.

Yes, churches that wish to grow must respect biblical principles. They will go astray in mere activism, statistical concern, or self-aggrandizement. But when they respect biblical principles, they can press forth under our sovereign God to vigorous growth, conscious that they are in the will of God and that what they are doing is pleasing to God—the one thing that matters!

QUESTIONS FOR REVIEW AND DISCUSSION

1. We suggest that the Scriptures are bubbling with Church Growth information, illustrations, principles, and priorities. Discuss the Scriptures in this light and begin a list which illustrates that statement.
2. How is the Bible "explained away" if lives of believers and their words do not agree?

3. Discuss the statement "Believers must become a part of the church; otherwise, the reality of their belief is in question."
4. How seriously does our church take the lostness of mankind in general and the lostness of mankind in our ministry area?
5. Christ said, "I will build my church"; yet he looks to believers to carry out that task. Discuss how God and man work together for the growth of his church.

3

Churches Grow As They Yield Themselves to God's Unswerving Purpose

Church growth begins in God's unswerving purpose to save men. Christ died on the cross and rose again that all families, kindreds, and classes of men might be discipled. Through Jesus Christ, God's intent was to open a way of salvation for all people whereby they might be reconciled to God. Freed from the power of sin and death, they would become parts of the reconciling Body of Christ—the church. This purpose of God, shared by his servants, is the driving force behind Church Growth. In his eternal purpose we ground our commitment to the multiplication of his churches throughout the world.

God's purpose for the growth of his church is affirmed, not in some isolated passages of Scripture, not in one book or portion of a chapter, but in Scripture in its entirety. God's intent to save men is the witness of the whole Bible.

Six passages help us focus clearly on God's unswerving purpose. Many more could serve to illustrate, but these six combined to sensitize the early church to its primary task of spreading the Good News and multiplying churches. These concepts must have been vivid in Paul's mind as he traveled around the Mediterranean planting churches. As these Scriptures pressed on the early church, and on the Apostle Paul, so should they press on us.

In the high priestly prayer, spoken at the Last Supper, Christ said, "As thou hast sent me into the world, even so have I also sent them into the world" (John 17:18). The purpose of the sending is clear. Five times in this prayer, the Lord expressed the idea that the basic purpose of his appointing and teaching and sending disciples was that "the world may believe." Telling men the Good News so convincingly that they believe on Christ is still the basic purpose of God's sending out servants today.

In his final earthly appearance to the disciples in Jerusalem, Christ said, "You will receive power when the Holy Spirit comes upon you; and you will bear witness for me in Jerusalem, and all over Judaea and Samaria, and away to the ends of the earth" (Acts 1:8, NEB). This directive, so contrary to what they expected, continued to stress the evangelization of the world. They expected Christ to restore the kingdom of Israel; he sent them out to evangelize the world. It's not our expectations that count; it is his directives.

A third indication of God's unswerving purpose came from the pen of the Apostle Paul: "God, who had set me apart from birth and called me through his grace, chose to reveal his Son to me and through me, in order that I might proclaim him among the Gentiles" (Gal. 1:16, NEB). The command was clear: "Proclaim him among the Gentiles." The date of that revelation to Paul was about A.D. 35. During the first huge expansion of Christianity and the mighty multiplication of churches throughout Jerusalem, Judea, Galilee, and Samaria, young Saul of Tarsus—a fanatical Jew—repeatedly heard Jewish Christians insist that the Lord Jesus had commanded the gospel to be proclaimed to all tribes and tongues, to everyone, to the ends of the earth.

As Saul persecuted the Christians, he asked angrily again and again, "Why do you keep going all over this country telling these innocent people about your wretched Jesus?" The Christians would reply, "Because the risen Jesus told us to tell everybody.

'Jerusalem, Judea, Samaria, and to the ends of the earth' were his exact words. He told us to; that is why we do it."

Ends of the earth—do you think they understood what that meant?

The simple Galilean Christians probably did not understand the whole import of the Lord's command to "disciple the peoples of earth," but Saul, the educated and traveled man, did. His first reaction was to hate the command which obviously denied that salvation was exclusively for the Jews. But after the risen Christ met him on the Damascus Road, Saul knew that God was calling him precisely to be a special messenger to the Gentiles, to the peoples of earth. He was to tell them that they could be saved without becoming Jews simply by believing on Jesus Christ. They had to *do* nothing. Works of righteousness were of no use.

Saul of Tarsus would never have accepted this utterly repugnant assignment, which ran counter to much of what was written in the law and the prophets and the psalms, except that it was the clear command of the Lord Jesus, both before and after his death and resurrection. What the Lord Jesus told him on the Damascus Road confirmed what Christians everywhere kept telling Saul that the Risen Lord had said. Saul yielded, made the 180-degree turn, and became missionary to the Gentiles.

The best recognized form of the Lord's command to disciple the peoples of the world is Matthew 28:19-20. This passage, the best-known version of the Great Commission, is only one of many Scripture verses which teach clearly that bringing men and women to intentional costly discipleship to Jesus Christ and membership in his church is a chief and irreplaceable duty and privilege of all Christians. "Go therefore and make disciples of all nations, baptizing them in the name of the Father and of the Son and of the Holy Spirit, teaching them to observe all that I have commanded you." Could anything be clearer?

Remember, the Great Commission in all its forms was a command to disciple *ta ethne*. Most English translations render this Greek phrase of Matthew 28:19 as "make disciples of all *nations*," but that is a mistranslation. *Ethne* does not mean "modern nation states" such as India, the United States, or China. *Ethne* means the castes, tribes, peoples, ethnic units of humankind. The Great Commission, flying like a banner over the church, constantly leads her on to disciple every piece of the vast mosaic of humankind, the three billion who have yet to believe. The tremendous multitudes who live around and beyond the reach of existing churches must be evangelized and discipled. This is the will of God, his unswerving purpose.

It is therefore inevitable that the Great Commission in various forms, voicing the eternal purpose of God our Savior, should appear again and again in the New Testament. It was marching orders for Christians.

In referring to his own call, Paul wrote, "This gospel, announced beforehand in sacred Scripture through the prophets [the Lord Jesus had carefully explained this to his disciples, see Luke 24:44] is about his son, Jesus Christ our Lord, through whom I received the privilege of a commission in his name *to bring to faith and obedience* men of all *ethne*" (see Rom. 1:-6). This verse is a command given to Saul, but surely it is a subhead under the great command.

Only because the church as a whole had been directed, beyond question, to disciple all tribes and castes and peoples, could Saul believe that he, who spoke Greek fluently and had been reared in a Greek city, was especially called of God to disciple the Gentiles.

A sixth version of the Great Commission is found in Romans 16:25–27: "To him who has power to make your standing sure, according to the Gospel I brought you and the proclamation of Jesus Christ, according to the revelation of that divine secret kept in silence for long ages but now disclosed, and through prophetic scriptures by eternal God's command made known to all nations, to bring them to faith and obedience—to God . . . be [the] glory" (NEB).

If from this complex, magnificent sentence we take the foundational thought, we read: "The Gospel, hidden for long ages, but now by eternal God's command made known to all *ethne* to bring them to faith and obedience." The gospel itself, this Scripture states, was disclosed by command of the everlasting God precisely to bring *ta ethne* (castes, classes, tribes, and people of earth) to faith in Jesus Christ and obedience to him!

The Great Commission in its various forms was no chance utterance. It was God's eternal purpose that all men have the opportunity to believe and be saved. It was part of the revelation of God through Jesus Christ our Lord which exerted (and was intended to exert) great pressure on the early church.

In its response to the Great Commission, why didn't the early church send missionaries to evangelize the world?

Men and women understand and respond according to their context. That is how first-century Christians understood and responded to this command of the Lord. It would be illogical for us to say, "When our Lord said so clearly, 'Preach the gospel to the ends of the earth,' he obviously meant Brazil, Greenland, Zambia, and Timbuktu. Therefore, the early church should have sent missionaries to all these lands. Since it did not, it probably did not know of the Great Commission."

Zambia and Timbuktu were not what the "ends of the earth" meant to those early disciples. The Galilean peasant-followers of our Lord had never been outside Palestine. To them, "the ends of the earth" meant Dan and Beersheba. That was where their world began and ended. Bound as they were by their intense Jewishness, they knew little about the rest of the globe. To the first Christians, the Great Commission, "discipling the *ethne*," meant discipling Judah and Benjamin and Levi—all the Jews then worshiping in the temple, living in Jerusalem, and working in Judea and Galilee. And disciple them they did!

Philip, remembering what the risen Lord had said, went to Samaria which, while near geographically, was at a great distance socially. He would never have gone to the Samaritans except for his Lord's express command—"Jerusalem, Judea, Samaria, and to the ends of the earth." In Samaria, the crowds listened eagerly to what Philip said. His ministry was blessed. Multitudes of Samaritans believed on the Lord Jesus Christ. At once, the Jerusalem churches sent Peter and John (not because they loved Samaritans but because the Lord had commanded "Samaria") who prayed for the converts, baptized all who believed, and added them to the church. With the Samaritan additions, the horizons of the church grew larger and larger. The early Christians' understanding of God's purpose grew.

The command of the Great Commission brought about the church's next great expansion which was *social*, not geographical. Scripture records that a great company of Levites—the priests (a separate endogamous tribe)—became obedient to the faith. This was a most unusual expansion. At first the Jerusalem and Judean churches were made up largely of common people. The apostles were considered "ignorant and unlearned men." For the most part, the middle-class people of Jerusalem stayed out of these "low-class" churches. A cultural, educational, and economic chasm yawned between upper-class Jews and many early Christians. These early Christians remembered the Lord's command and continued to pray for the salvation of their "upper-class" neighbors. They continued to witness to them and to endure their scorn. They kept sharing the new life in Christ. Then "a great company of the priests" became obedient to Christ. They were baptized and added to the church. These priests brought into the churches a larger view. They were men of learning and saw new meaning in Christ's command to preach the gospel to all peoples. The church's understanding of the Great Commission was expanded. Christians began to see the possibilities and to believe that they had an obligation to Jews in other lands around the Mediterranean. Evangelism continued and churches were born. The understanding expanded again, and large numbers of proselytes became Christians. Another great segment of society opened to the Good News.

The Great Commission continued pressing on Christians and churches in Jerusalem, Judea, Samaria, Antioch, Corinth, and

Ephesus. The vision extended, the horizon expanded, and Gentiles were added to the church. Paul, of course, played a key role in perceiving the true and wider meaning of the Great Commission. House churches by the hundreds arose with no Jews whatever in their membership.

Then implementing the Great Commission was interrupted for about two hundred years as the churches of the Roman world interpreted "the world" to mean the Latin-Greek civilization in and near the cities. Scripture was available in Greek and later in Latin. Cities became strongly Christian, and countrysides remained non-Christian. Actually, the word *pagan* originally meant "country people" because those who lived in villages continued as pagans and worshiped idols. They generally spoke some tribal dialect rather than Latin or Greek. Christianity won the city people but stopped short at the linguistic and cultural barriers between them and the peasantry. Christians in the cities understood the Great Commission to mean "Go into all the Latin and Greek world and disciple the people there." They obeyed the Great Commission as they understood it, according to their context, and the cities of the world became largely Christian.

Did that same principle hold true in later periods?

In each period, the Great Commission was seen and obeyed in its context. In the sixteenth century the Reformers—Luther, Calvin, and others—all but forgot world evangelization. One could easily believe that the Reformers thought the Great Commission expired with the apostles. They had important work to do in Europe, and access to the rest of the non-Christian world was completely cut off. Sea lanes to the west and south were controlled by Roman Catholics of Spain and Portugal. Land roads to the south and east were controlled by Moslems. Consequently, the Reformers believed that "the ends of the world" meant Ireland, North Italy, and the northern tip of Spain, the ends of their world. It would be wrong to impose twentieth-century standards on

Christians of former ages. We need to see what the "ends of the earth" looked like to them and praise them for their courageous convictions which often resulted in martyrdom.

Since the days of the apostles, distance has diminished enormously and knowledge expanded explosively. With supersonic travel and jets, "my neighborhood" has expanded to take in the *whole world*. "My neighbors" have become *all* people throughout the world. Instantaneously, by satellite, I see "my neighbors" in my front room; I am an eye witness to their hurt and hunger, wars and woes, loneliness and lostness. Decisions made in one country about oil, economics, and nuclear weapons affect all countries. So do decisions to accept or reject Christ. Christians must understand that the fact of "one world" lays upon them awesome responsibility in fulfilling the Great Commission. It has always been the unswerving purpose of God to save the whole world. Now, as Christians, God's vision must be our vision too!

The world's population now numbers four billion people; approximately three billion are non-Christians, and one billion, Christians. By the year A.D. 2000, a short time from now, there will be some six billion people; approximately four billion will be non-Christian. Against this backdrop the church of Jesus Christ must hear the Lord's command: "Disciple the peoples of earth." Against this backdrop the church of Jesus Christ must measure its obedience and see its enormous opportunities!

Do you see today's church responding to this opportunity?

To illustrate the contemporary meaning of the Great Commission, let us look at the United States. We are commanded to disciple *ta ethne*. What does this mean to this country? What does it mean to the sixty-four million practicing, active Christians in the United States? For purposes of analysis we will divide the two hundred fifteen million Americans into three segments. Three different kinds of evangelism (E-0, E-1, and E-2) are needed to reach these multitudes.

First, there is the group of people whom we shall call "assimilated Americans," those who view themselves in the mainstream of American culture. Enormous numbers of them belong to some church or denomination but their commitment to Jesus Christ is vague and ineffectual. They live from day to day with little consciousness of obedience to a Master. They consider themselves Christians but do not really know what being "in Christ" means. They tend to grow more and more alienated and secular. They have little consciousness of betraying Christ or disobeying their Shepherd, but they are living without a Shepherd, and they acknowledge no Lord.

In every community, large numbers of assimilated Americans claim the name *Christian* but know little or nothing of Christ's power. Perhaps they were baptized years ago, but they cannot remember when or where. As children, they may have gone to Sunday school. They attended a church—was it Methodist, Catholic, or Baptist?—some years ago in New York—or was it Alabama or California? They believe in God the creator. Their names were once on a church roll, and they will want a minister to officiate at their funerals, but they are not practicing Christians. Yet they feel uneasy about their relationship to God and think they will do something about it—sometime!

This group of nominal or marginal Christians numbers approximately seventy-one million. This is one contemporary context in which the church must understand the Great Commission. We are directed to win to Christ this huge segment of the American population, and they are very winnable!

But aren't you talking about "sheep stealing"?

One of the most common explanations that nongrowth churches or denominations give for growing churches is that they steal sheep. Sometimes the charge is leveled against Pentecostals, Seventh Day Adventists, Baptists, or Roman Catholics. What is the substance of this allegation?

Millions of neglected "Christians" live all around us. Any church that runs an attractive, agressive program will attract some

of these people away from other churches. The process goes on all
the time. When a member disagrees with his fellow members,
board, or minister, he often stops attending and joins another
church. Conversely, a neighbor says to Mrs. T., "Do visit our
church. We have such a lovely choir and such warm fellowship."
As the friendship develops, Mrs. T. drops out of her old church
and becomes a member of the other. This coming and going is a
perpetual process.

On the whole, it is a good thing. People ought to be free to
worship God wherever they wish, and churches ought to serve
their members well. When the standard of service gets low, members leave and go to other churches. Automatic pruning helps
keep churches active and dutiful. The pastor does not want a
captive audience that has to take whatever he gives them. It keeps
the pastor on his toes to know that while he is free to preach the
Word as he sees it his people are also free to worship elsewhere if
they feel he is unbiblical or not challenging enough.

A church has much to gain and little to lose by maintaining that
personal choice and conviction keeps any member worshiping in
one congregation rather in some other. Religious freedom is precious and easily lost.

Opposition to this view was fathered by the state churches of
Europe. In these, men and women "belonged" to the church in
the same way that peasants belonged to the feudal lord. They were
born into a church—Lutheran, Presbyterian, Anglican, or Roman
Catholic—and it was sinful (they were taught) to join another
denomination. Any pastor who tried to attract them was sheep
stealing. Freedom of religion and conscience did not exist. Being
baptized in infancy was similar to the practice of branding calves;
from that point on a person *belonged* to the denomination, and woe
betide anyone who took him or her into another.

Well-fed sheep cannot be stolen. Convinced Christians stay in
their churches. They steadily refuse to join other congregations.
In fact, one may say that if sheep can be stolen the practice is not
sheep stealing. Finding sheep running wild in the streets or hun-

gry on the mountainside and bringing them back to the fold is not sheep stealing. It is engaging in Christ's work of finding and folding the lost. Furthermore, charges of sheep stealing are usually exaggerated.

One should not understand this to mean condoning a mean-spirited raiding of other congregations. It is sin to disturb the faith of Christians who are happily a part of another church unless one gives them something more biblical. Getting Christians to change affiliation without their gaining any deeper understanding of the Lord or becoming any more obedient to him is a condemnable procedure.

During the past fifty years, most pastors in North America have leaned over backward to avoid the charge of sheep stealing. Partly as a result of this, about seventy-one million assimilated Americans are nominal, marginal, or slightly lapsed Christians. What is now demanded is that every congregation seek to be a better community, to have more biblical teaching, warmer fellowship, more Christian love, more concern for social justice, and more effective evangelism of the lost. When a prospect says, "I belong to another church," he or she ought to be asked as kindly as possible, "Are you a practicing Christian? Do you know and love Christ?" If the answers to these questions are not satisfactory, he or she (a sheep running wild on the range) ought to be found, folded, fed, and transformed.

If this is sheep stealing, let us steal boldly!

Evangelism Zero (E-o) is used to win nominal Christians—baptized "unbelievers"—back to fervent faith. It is often more "renewal" than evangelism. Hence, we call it Evangelism Zero (E-o).

Does finding neglected, careless Christians exhaust the meaning of the Great Commission for Americans?

No, there is a second great block of the American population, and a second great meaning in today's context. Consider the large number of assimilated Americans who do not belong to any church, nor consider themselves Christians. In America they number approximately thirty-six million. They are fellow Democrats or Republicans. They live on our streets. They meet us on the golf course. They sell the stock we buy. Most are very nice people, but they would not be offended if they were described as "pagans." They have openly rejected Christianity as untenable for modern man. They avidly believe that life was created, not of course by God, but by just the right mix of methane gas and other elements swirling round at a conveniently correct temperature. They are hard-core secularists and humanists. Others who claim no relationship to Christ are hedonists; they earnestly pursue pleasure. They have an invincible belief that if they try hard enough, get enough education, and make and spend enough money all their problems will be solved and life will be a lot of fun!

In America, these unbelieving pagans are raw material for Evangelism One. They are winnable but not as winnable as E-o people. Many are distinctly resistant. When these assimilated Americans are converted, they feel comfortable in churches made up of fellow assimilated Americans. Their culture, language, education, and income are compatible with that of most middle-class Americans.

Lost people in both categories total about one hundred and seven million in the United States, and prayer is urgently needed for them. Every congregation should focus its teaching and preaching on these spiritually starved multitudes who are living on a much lower level than God desires. Incalculable needs and opportunities for Evangelism Zero (E-o) and Evangelism One (E-1) lie all about us.

The third main segment of the two hundred fifteen million and the third main contemporary meaning of the Great Commission arises from the millions of Americans who are culturally distinctive and are self-consciously so. They are Americans who maintain a cultural, and sometimes linguistic, practice which arises from the ethnic and cultural heritage of their forebears. These minorities—Koreans, Arabs, Lebanese, Chinese, Portuguese, Puerto Ricans, Argentineans, Mexicans, Japanese, Asian Indians, Africans, and on and on—are part of the rich and multistranded fabric of American society.

Many individuals in these groups, of course, are ardent Christians, walking in the Light, feeding on the Word, and propagating the gospel. About fourteen million of these are included in the sixty-four million active Christians. They do not need to be evangelized; they evangelize.

The balance of these culturally distinctive multitudes are either nominal Christians or confessedly not Christian. In both cases they need to hear and obey the gospel. They ought to be discipled. They are winnable.

It is difficult to determine how many people fall into this classification because members of these groups are continually merging into the general American population. Third and fourth-generation Spanish Americans, Chinese, and Italians are part of our pluralistic American society. Yet we estimate that there are fifty-eight million culturally distinct Americans. If we assume fourteen million of these are practicing Christians, that leaves about forty-four million ethnic sheep who are not responsible, practicing Christians in any denomination. Thirty-four million of these may be nominals. Ten million of them may not really be Christians at all.

A table will help us see the proportions of these different elements in the general American population of two hundred fifteen million in 1976.

	Assimilated Americans	Culturally Distinct Americans
Active, Practicing Christians	50 million	14 million
Nominal, Marginal Christians	71 million	34 million
No Claim to Be Christian	36 million	10 million
Total	157 million +	58 million = 215 million

We shall not quarrel with anyone who estimates these numbers differently.* Whatever figures are quoted, enormous numbers of culturally distinct Americans need Christ—as of course do assimilated Americans.

Most ethnic minorities are also linguistic units. At home and among close friends and family, they speak their own language or dialect. That may be Spanish, Korean, Navajo, or Hungarian. They are conscious of being culturally distinct from other Americans. They sometimes become members of congregations of assimilated Americans, but the adjustment is difficult. They think of themselves as different. The Great Commission presses on today's churches as we gaze upon millions of ethnics who are not yet ardent Christians.

How can ethnics be won?

Evangelism Two (E-2) is demanded. This is evangelism across a small but distinct culture barrier. Ideally, E-2 creates new congregations in the ethnic unit being evangelized. Among Arabs, it creates Arab churches. Among Mexicans, it creates Mexican churches. Among Chinese, it creates Chinese churches. E-2 is not "near-neighbor evangelism," bringing converts into white Anglo-Saxon protestant congregations. Church planters using Evangelism Two must learn a new language, create new congregations in ethnic units, nurture them, and, as fast as possible, build up indigenous leadership within them.

---

*Such estimates are beset with difficulties. Who is an active practicing Christian? A born-again Christian? Should a nominal, whose name is on the church roll but never gives, be listed in the second great block of Americans—those who do not consider themselves Christians? Are all those to be called Christian who have been baptized in infancy? If one has attended church in the last month, may it be presumed that he is an active Christian? How nominal must a person be before he is placed in the third group—No Claim to Be Christian? Such questions can be answered in several ways. The pastor with a shepherd heart will reply in one way; the scientific-minded Christian in another. The one defending his flock from decline will reply in one way; the shepherd searching for lost sheep in another.

While E-2 creates culturally distinct churches, it must, at the same time, build brotherhood. It must neither advocate nor allow segregation. It is creating culture and language churches solely as a convenience to ethnics who operate most effectively in that culture and language. Ethnic congregations should usually be part of a denomination in which there are many types of congregations —all equal and all regarding the others as brothers and sisters in Christ.

The fourth contemporary context facing today's Christian is a great block of humanity that lives at a tremendous cultural, linguistic, and usually geographic distance from most American Christians. At least three billion non-Christians (Hindus, Buddhists, Marxists, Moslems, Animists) have yet to believe on Jesus Christ. Most have yet to hear his name in any meaningful way.

To evangelize these huge populations, all congregations and churches in all countries will have to engage in E-3. They will have to send missionaries who learn other languages and who thoroughly become a part of those lands and those cultures, missionaries who patiently commend Christ by word and deed across major linguistic and cultural barriers.

We can measure our evangelistic thrust and effectiveness in a rather simple way. How many members does it take to send out a full-time evangelistic worker? (When one works within his or her own culture, he or she is called a church planter. When one crosses cultural barriers, he or she is called a missionary.) In some American denominations it takes five thousand members to send one evangelistic worker. In other denominations, it takes one thousand. In a few dedicated denominations, it takes one hundred members to send one evangelistic worker.

Church Growth is not optional; it is commanded of God. In the last quarter of the twentieth century, the unswerving purpose of our Lord to save men, voiced so frequently in the New Testament and seen in light of these four contemporary contexts, means that growth must be our goal. Churches must grow by *expansion* of existing congregations and by *extension* in establishing new congregations. Churches must grow by winning to Christ:

1. assimilated Americans who are nominal Christians—E-0
2. assimilated Americans who are confessed non-Christians—E-1
3. culturally distinct Americans who are not believing, practicing Christians—E-2
4. very different kinds of people, mostly in other lands, who have yet to hear and believe—E-3

All four kinds of evangelism are required of all Christians by God's unchanging mandate.

Establishing a congregation of the redeemed in every community, in every neighborhood, of every class and condition of people is what our Father has sent us here to do.

Let us be about his business!

QUESTIONS FOR REVIEW AND DISCUSSION

1. Does our perspective change when we see the Great Commission in light of *ta ethne*?
2. Explore and discuss in greater detail the scriptural references in this chapter.
3. If throughout history people have understood and responded to the Great Commission in their own context, what is the response in our context today?
4. Identify the kinds of people within the church's ministry area who could be reached through E-0, E-1, E-2.
5. What steps might be taken to focus evangelistic efforts on each group?
6. What new ideas and insights have you discovered in the section dealing with "sheep stealing"?

4

Churches Grow As Priority Is Given to Effective Evangelism

A Church Growth definition of *evangelism* is "to proclaim Jesus Christ as God and Savior, to persuade people to become his disciples and responsible members of his church." Understanding the various elements in this definition provides an in-depth perspective on effective evangelism.

Responsible member. The church is the Body of Christ, and the responsible member is part of that Body. When the Body functions as it should, each part maintains communication with the head, constantly sending and receiving messages. Christ is the head of the Body; responsible members get directions from him. Their behavior as part of his Body should exemplify how Christ functions in the world. A responsible member would be acutely aware of the unchurched and the unsaved, those who live without knowing Jesus Christ or his power, joy, forgiveness, and love.

A responsible member carries his or her share of the church's work—giving, worshiping, and working happily with other members.

A responsible member discovers where he or she fits in the Body, which is composed of many parts, each having its place. The Apostle Paul wrote that when each part works as it should, the whole Body *grows*. God gives gifts to Christians for evangelism and ministry. As individual Christians discover their gifts and use them, the Body functions as it was meant to function. The lost are seen—and found. Discovering and using one's gifts is part of being a responsible member.

A responsible member lives in the world as a Christian. The surroundings of some parts of the Body of Christ often have social, economic, educational, and governmental aspects that are displeasing to God. The responsible member endeavors to change these and to bring God's mercy and justice to bear on this distorted world.

To summarize, being a "responsible member," then, includes: (1) the Christian's own relationship to Jesus Christ, the Head of the Body; (2) his sharing in the life and work of the local church; (3) his consciously discovering and using the gifts God gives him so that the church grows; and (4) his endeavoring to change what is displeasing to God and bring peace, justice, love, and brotherhood into the world.

His disciple. Church Growth people believe effective evangelism means making disciples and responsible members of Christ's church. Many methods of evangelism emphasize making *decisions.* Church Growth people are concerned with making *disciples.*

Surveys among Christian people show that approximately half cannot recall a moment of definite "decision for Christ." While they live in commitment and relationship to Jesus Christ, they cannot rmember a particular time, place, or circumstance when they made a "decision."

Whether or not one can remember the initial step, becoming a disciple means continually living with the Lord, walking with him, and learning from him. The disciple becomes familiar with God's Word. He walks worthy of his high calling. He is in contact with the Lord. Being a disciple means bringing one's habits, thoughts, emotions, feelings, and expenditure of money and time under the control of his Master Jesus Christ.

But what about decisions?

A decision is often the first step. However, we deceive ourselves if we believe that a person who has made a decision for Christ, who has prayed, "I accept Jesus Christ into my life," has truly become a disciple. We must make sure that he or she really follows Christ, really lives as a disciple. The goal is that day by day, hour by hour, minute by minute, one lives yielded to Christ as a responsible part of the Body. This is what it means to be a disciple.

A *decision* suggests a brief moment of time; a *disciple* suggests a lifelong task. The word *decision* inadequately describes the lifelong commitment called for in Scripture. We do well to use the more biblical concept of disciple and to evaluate our effectiveness in that context.

Proclamation and persuasion.

Churches grow when priority is given to effective evangelism, which includes "proclamation and persuasion." *Proclamation* is telling people by word and deed, of Jesus the Savior. But we not only proclaim him as Savior, we counter people's objections and present him in a way they can understand. We proclaim Christ in the "heart language" of the person, in his or her dialect, vocabulary, way of thinking, income, and education. These and other considerations are taken into account by the proclaimer and persuader.

The Good News will be spread among six million French Canadians chiefly by Christians who think French Canadian, dream French Canadian, talk French Canadian, and live in French Canada. The Christians will build French Canadian churches in which deacons, elders, and members are French Canadian. When that happens, we will begin to make a real impact on the French Canadian community. A similar illustration could be given for each group of people in every region of the world.

But why must God's Word be adapted to the cultural setting to be effective?

When one physically hears the Word, it doesn't penetrate the "inner ear" unless it's in his or her frame of reference. The Word is not given a fair hearing unless the receiver can hear it without any "friction" and can accept it without encountering annoying "static" which frequently blocks effective communication.

One can proclaim to a pagan university professor in his or her native language, but he or she will not really get the message unless it is in his or her "heart language."

Isn't it God's business to persuade? If we are faithful in telling the story, the rest is up to the Holy Spirit.

When Titus came back from Macedonia, he found Paul in the Corinthian synagogues arguing and "persuading." There is a good biblical basis for assuming that God frequently persuades through us. If we sit quietly in our corner and refuse to persuade, we are actually being disobedient to the Holy Spirit. We are refusing to follow God's leading. We should build persuasion right into our evangelism. Without persuasion, without intending for people to become disciples of Jesus Christ, evangelism is a thin, anemic substitute for the real thing. Persuasion is an essential part of effective evangelism.

Aren't you bordering on arm twisting? Don't you violate people's rights if you persuade?

That danger is very much overestimated. The normal human being has a great ability to resist persuasion. For example, most people see and hear powerful persuasion on television and turn it off completely. People can turn off Christian persuasion just as easily.

We should be courteous, of course, and sensitive to other people's feelings. We do not advocate that Christians persuade so vigorously and so crudely that people become antagonized. That would be not only counterproductive but sub-Christian. However, courteously, intelligently, lovingly persuading people is an essential of effective evangelism and should be a vital part of our Christian expression.

But if we live the Christian life, others will see it and be attracted to Christ and his church. Isn't that enough?

Scripture teaches two kinds of evangelism. The first is *attraction*. The quality of believers' lives is such that people are drawn to the church. Many times movements to Christ develop because non-Christians see the attractive quality of life in believers. As responsible members of the church radiate the joy of Christ and exhibit the fruit of the Spirit, people are attracted.

The second kind of evangelism is *proclamation*. The Son of man came to *seek* and to save; the seventy were sent forth to *tell*; the Apostle Paul proclaimed the gospel; the early Christians went everywhere spreading the gospel. Proclamation is an important type of biblical evangelism.

A caution must be voiced in regard to evangelism by *attraction*. Some churches are so friendly, warm, and loving that people are attracted to them rather than to Christ. Christians have their treasures in earthen vessels. Christ is our treasure; we are clay pots. We proclaim *not ourselves* but Christ. No matter how good we are, we are still earthen vessels. We should be proclaiming the treasure in the earthen vessels, that is, Christ in us, the hope of glory.

Remember too that while "unintentional evangelism" (what evangelism by attraction essentially is) is good, it is limited. The only people we touch are those few with whom we are in close contact. We cannot be responsible members of the Body unless we practice "intentional evangelism." Our *purpose* must be to win those who are living without the treasure.

In India, the great Gandhi once said to some missionaries, "You work so hard at it. Just remember that the rose never invites anyone to smell it. If it is fragrant, people will walk across the garden and endure the thorns to smell it." He was really saying, "Try to be more roselike and less evangelistic." Gandhi was mistaken. The Christian is not a rose, unconcerned over whether or not it gives joy. The Christian is a part of the Body of Christ. One should, of course, be as charming and delightful and "fragrant" as possible, but the Christian must also deliberately intend that through his or her life and conscious witness people will become inheritors of eternal and abundant life.

What do you mean by priority in effective evangelism?

After studying hundreds of churches, it is clear that few are actually structured for growth. In fact, many are structured for nongrowth. They give low priority to evangelism. A simple way to discover where a church places its priority is to draw a bar-graph showing how that church spends its money. The budget is usually a good indicator as to what a church thinks is really important. A graph will usually reveal that a static church spends large amounts for salaries, maintenance, mortgages, and materials but a small amount for outreach and evangelism, especially for local evangelistic ministry. Such bar-graphs usually illustrate how little a church invests in *its own growth*.

Another indicator of priority for evangelism is the church staff. Who is the second staff person chosen after the pastor? A youth director? A religious education director? A music director? Each of these positions is important; but, for the church placing priority on effective evangelism, the next person on the staff should work in evangelism/church growth. When a staff person giving 365 days a year to evangelism, the possibilities for growth increase measurably.

Such a staff person, if he is effective in evangelism and in enabling others, will soon have enlarged the present congregation to the place where his salary is completely underwritten by the income received from new members. This is usually not the case when the second person on the staff is a youth director or a Christian education director.

The pastor must begin thinking about the priority of evangelism and encourage people to see for themselves what it will mean. The congregation will often discover meanings the pastor had not considered. The priority of evangelism has its basis in God's will. We must ask, "What priorities does the head of the church desire?" This is an important question to be asked by every pastor, church, and denomination.

Isn't it true that if our church could first be renewed then evangelism would automatically follow?

We would like to answer in the affirmative, to say, "Yes, the only thing you need do is renew your church, and it will automatically grow," but this is just not true. Some of the best churches, the most orthodox, the most charming, the most intelligent, and most renewed, grow the least. Renewal, in and of itself, is no guarantee of growth. Renewal is a good thing. One could scarcely have too much. We all need to live in greater contact with the Savior, to know more of the Scripture, and to be more yielded. However, unless our renewal results in winning the lost, in giving first priority to time to share Christ, it is ingrown and falls short of what Christ requires.

Renewal should take place before, during, and after evangelism. The church is constantly in need of renewal. However, we cannot accept the idea that the existing church is so carnal it can do no evangelism. If that were the case, there would never be any evangelism. The church must start where it is and evangelize from there. Evangelism should take place all the time—before, during, and after renewal. The true church evangelizes and renews itself simultaneously.

Do you equate renewal and revival?

Each word has its own connotation, but, in large measure, they are substantially the same. A number of interesting studies have shown that some churches have been revived and have grown and that other churches have been revived and *did not* grow. People in the latter group enjoyed themselves, forgave one another, and reinstituted communication. The Holy Spirit descended, but the churches didn't grow.

Rejoice with churches that are revived; rejoice with churches that are renewed. Yet make sure that the renewal or revival results in the people of God, who have experienced this change, reaching the lost, persuading people to become Christians, and investing time in evangelism until the Lord adds daily to his church.

Have you heard the proposal that if we were Spirit-filled Christians we would evangelize? We wouldn't need a plan to evangelize; God would direct us.

This thinking could be a significant stumbling block in evangelizing North America and indeed the world. We should be sensitive to the Spirit's leading, and we should be Spirit-filled, but a firm Church Growth conviction is that one of the earliest manifestations of being Spirit-filled is to do definite, conscious evangelism. If a person claiming to be Spirit-filled is not evangelizing, one must doubt how full he or she is and wonder what kind of spirit he or she is full of.

If a person is full of the spirit of Christ, he will be tremendously concerned for the unevangelized—both those near to him and those far away. The spirit of Christ is concerned that men and women come to salvation. When we are full of his spirit, we will be telling others the Good News.

How does one plan for effective evangelism?

An effective plan does not limit itself to an evangelistic campaign once every other year or so but builds constant evangelism into the life of the local church. Week after week, month after month, year after year, people are discipled and become responsible members.

Effective evangelism comes as each church develops those qualities of life, attributes of the Spirit, and understandings of the Word which naturally lead members without any sense of reluctance into evangelistic work. Evangelism becomes their joy; it is a normal expression of their lives. Achieving this kind of evangelism means structuring Church Growth at every level—in the board, in the women's fellowships, in youth groups, in Christian education, and through every part of the Body.

You use the word effective. *Behind that seems to lurk the implication that not everything we do is going to be effective. Are some evangelistic methods more effective than others?*

No question! Part of the problem is that many churches are using evangelistic methods that don't work. Perhaps they worked some place else or some years ago or were part of denominational practice. These churches never raise the question as to whether the same methods are effective today. For example, one denomination never has a church service without giving an invitation. Fifty years ago that was standard practice and brought a constant stream of converts into the church. Today it does not bring many; yet this method has a certain sanctified aura which leads it to be continued year after year without results.

We must constantly inquire, Are the methods we use actually communicating the gospel? If the answer is yes, continue using them; if no, discard them and find methods that do. Any living church should be continually testing evangelistic methods. Some will work for one church and not for another. Some worked last year but won't work this year. The church must constantly experiment and evaluate. It must constantly ask if people are actually being added to the church.

Effective evangelism is a "mix" of many factors that in themselves might not be effective but together produce God-honoring, effective evangelism. The "mix" is important. Until a church finds the right combination, its evangelism will probably not be very effective.

A Methodist missionary to Bolivia spoke of this "mix" some years ago. He called it "the right proportion of ingredients," using the analogy of making a cake. The cake isn't all flour, all sugar, all eggs, or all butter; it is the right mix of these ingredients. When you have the right mix, you have a wonderful cake. If you have the wrong mix, you have a flat, hard piece of dough. The same is true of evangelism. When you get the right "mix," the right proportion of concern, biblical authority, attractive witness, caring for people, speaking the common language, addressing the message within culture, and many other factors, you have effective evangelism.

Church Growth principles are parts of the mix. The ingredients include a right understanding of how a congregation has grown or has not grown, the community in which it lives with its various parts, and the receptivity of each part. Every principle in this book is part of the "mix," and as you work your way through the chapters, you should ask, How much of this particular ingredient should we use in our "mix"?

To be effective, evangelism must produce results; otherwise, as Paul said, "It is beating the air," only shadowboxing. The right "mix," however, produces effective evangelism. People will respond to Christ, and the church will grow.

QUESTIONS FOR REVIEW AND DISCUSSION

1. Discuss the following key words as they apply to your church: persuading, disciples, responsible members.
2. Evaluate your church's ministry through evangelism by attraction and evangelism by persuasion.
3. If it's God's will that his church grow that that lost people are found, is it possible that a church which is not growing is out of God's will? Discuss the implications.
4. A spirit-filled church makes definite, concrete plans for evangelism. Enumerate the concrete plans for evangelism in your church.
5. Evangelism "mix" is extremely important. Discuss this "mix" as it relates to your church.

5

Churches Grow As They Rightly Discern the Body

As we consider various factors and principles relating to Church Growth, we need abundant, accurate information about the members of our churches. This basic principle of Church Growth is called *Discerning the Body*. Pastors and lay people need to discern the Body in the congregation in which they are serving. For this, Church Growth eyes are essential.

An accurate understanding of the Body of Christ, discerned reverently and described scientifically, assists Christian leaders in being good stewards of the grace of God and effective communicators of the gospel of Christ.

The Body of Christ is the church, of which your church and my church are parts. The church as it grows anywhere always grows in specific congregations; it never grows in general. Growth occurs as specific congregations increase their membership (expansion) and as churches plant new congregations (extension). The church grows in the countryside, metropolis, inner city, suburbs, exurbia, and among many different kinds of people. Each individual congregation is established and grows in its own milieu.

The Body of Christ—the church—is a concrete entity. It is made up of countable people, and there is nothing spiritual in not counting them. The Body is identifiable as members, churches, associations, and denominations. Christians must be concerned with the Body, with winning men to Christ, incorporating them into the Body, and multiplying congregations. If we fail in this, then one day there will be no Body. The church is continually dying; therefore, there must be continual reproduction. Great numbers of non-Christians throughout America can and must be won into existing churches and by the planting of new churches.

As discerning Christians, it is our business to know everything possible about the Body. The Body needs to be described accurately. The Body needs to be described scientifically. The Body needs to be described in its various parts. The reason, we repeat, is that an accurate understanding of the Body of Christ, discerned reverently and described scientifically, aids Christians in becoming good stewards of the grace of God and effective communicators of the Gospel of Christ.

Dr. Merton Alexander has made an analogy relating the Body of Christ to the human body. For many years, he carried on a double ministry. His practice in California afforded him enough money to travel to Africa, where he ran a mission hospital for six months out of every year. Upon returning to the United States he resumed his practice.

Dr. Alexander is an ardent Church Growth man. In an article in *Church Growth Bulletin* he stated:

> Being of a scientific frame of mind, through medicine, and seeing the human body as a doctor must, I draw analogies from our physical body concerning the Body of Christ. What catalyzed the Renaissance was the climate of thought permitted by the ecclesiastical authorities of that time. The Renaissance held that one could, without intruding into divinely forbidden areas, look into natural phenomenon seeking natural causes for natural effects. Modern medicine rests on the assumption that it is permissible and necessary to behold the Body, even if it is the Temple of the living God. I permit myself to see abnormalities as well as normalities in The Body. The Perfect Life, who once walked the Judean hills and the Perfect Spirit who now indwells the Body, encourage me to dream of the day when all segments of the Body (homogeneous units we call them in Church Growth) will be

filled with the glow of perfect good health. For after all, the Church is the normal Body of Christ.

Such an analogy crystalizes our thinking of the church we serve and elevates our concepts of the church. We should think of Church Growth in terms of extending and perfecting the normal Body of Christ.

How does one go about discerning the Body?

Discerning the Body begins with Church Growth eyes. Unfortunately, this is what many leaders, many Christians, do not have. As soon as one concentrates attention on discerning and describing the existing church, he or she sees one significant reason for the lack of church growth—a lack of Church Growth conscience. This is why some congregations are not sharing in the growth God is granting to many others.

Some Christians, both laymen and ministers, are just not interested in Church Growth. They envision themselves doing something more important! They have no conscience on Church Growth, and usually their congregations are experiencing little growth. This disinterest is partly because they don't see their church accurately in all its parts—growth history, present condition, and potential.

Each church grows in different ways and has a different growth potential, and the potential of the same church will be different at different times. History illustrates this truth. Over two hundred years ago, Shuble Stern, a Baptist minister, founded the Sandy Creek Baptist Church in Randolph County, North Carolina. In those days Baptists were relatively unknown. Within seventeen years that church had become mother, grandmother, and great-grandmother to forty-two other churches, and 125 ministers had gone forth from these churches to serve.

The same truth is illustrated in urban Manhattan in a more contemporary setting. In 1956 Manhattan Baptist Church began as a house fellowship on Twenty-third Street in New York City. Paul James, the pastor of a three-thousand-member Baptist

Church in Atlanta, Georgia, resigned to become pastor of the newly organized Manhattan Baptist Church. In its first six years, Manhattan Baptist founded sixteen daughter churches. When a church sees itself accurately and realizes its growth potential, the Body grows.

Every congregation and every denomination should take growth history and growth potential seriously. Developing Church Growth eyes helps one see such opportunities.

With all this "opportunity," why is there so little growth?

Lack of holy living, lack of fervent prayer, lack of correct doctrine, lack of brotherly love are commonly mentioned as reasons for lack of Church Growth. A reason not so commonly named is that the Body is not clearly seen and not accurately described. Church Growth is seldom a part of ordinary conversations, seldom discussed by church leaders, and seldom mentioned in prayer. Christians seldom agonize before God concerning the growth of their churches.

Christians live in a universal fog concerning Church Growth. Many ministers are scarcely aware of Church Growth. They carry on programs, preach sermons, raise budgets, and conduct funerals year after year without ever being acutely conscious of the patterns and forms of growth or nongrowth that exist in their congregations.

A few years ago, I, Dr. McGavran, was studying the growth of the Presbyterian Church in Taiwan. This denomination grew rapidly for a few years, declined, then plateaued for twenty years, and then grew again quite rapidly. That was the record I gleaned from the annual statistics, but I didn't know what had caused this pattern. I searched various sources and reports with no results. Then what I thought was a gold mine fell into my hands—the official minutes of the Presbyterian Church and Mission in Taiwan for that whole period.

"My search is over," I said. "I will read these minutes and find the reasons." I read every word of those twenty-two hundred minutes. There was information about when missionaries came to the field, when they went home on sick leave, buying property, a case of immorality in the boys' boarding school, white-washing the doctor's kitchen, and on and on. But there wasn't a single paragraph about why the church had grown, declined, plateaued, and then grown again.

I was thinking some hard thoughts about my Presbyterian friends when the Lord said to me, "Donald, you sat on the executive committee of the Indian Mission of the Disciples of Christ for twenty-five years, didn't you?"

I said, "Yes, Sir."

He said, "How much time did you spend describing the growth or nongrowth of your church?"

How much time did we spend? How much time do we spend in our board meetings illustrating the past growth of our church, its growth potential, its problem areas, or the things that need to be done? Failure to rightly understand the Body, discern it reverently, and describe it scientifically causes a fog which obscures the facts.

Speaking of "fog," what are the causes and how do you remove them?

Some causes are psychological, and possibly the biggest is "sour grapes." Christian churches that are not growing are just not interested in growth. They indulge in defensive thinking, in rationalization. Sour-grape Christians maintain that Church Growth is what less reputable denominations are interested in. "Reputable denominations like *ours*," they say, "are neither getting growth nor, thank God, expecting to get it. We respectable denominations are concerned about something more important!" Or they say, "Big churches can get it but not little churches like ours." Or, "Little churches can grow, but big established churches like ours can't expect to."

Sour-grape thinking represents excuses and defensive thinking,

and it is particularly harmful when we "canonize" it and quote
Scripture to support it. Once we give way to that kind of thinking, we literally cannot see Church Growth. It is hidden from us
by a swirling fog that envelops us.

Another psychological cause of the fog in many sections of the
world is the cooperative spirit which causes many churches to
relax. Dr. Robert Schuller of the Garden Grove Community
Church in Southern California, discussed this cause in *Your
Church Has Real Possibilities*:

> "There should be no hostility or proselyting of members of another
> church, but the co-operative spirit that causes any church to relax
> becomes failure prone. I tell people that I work as if our church were
> the only church of Jesus Christ in all of Orange County and that the
> salvation of all the half million souls there depended upon us alone."*

That is good thinking, the kind of thinking every church should
do.

Theological causes also add to the fog. The religious relativism
so common in America arises from our pluralistic society in
which many different kinds of people are equal before the law and
are guaranteed religious liberty. In this society it is easy for men to
jump to the erroneous conclusion that all religions are equally
good. Anyone who thinks that way is really in the fog.

A second theological cause is elevating unity above salvation.
Within the Christian community we are—and should be—cooperative with other Christians. From that good base we edge over
into error. We come to believe that every person even vaguely
connected with another denomination, whether or not he or she
knows Jesus Christ, is a Christian. No endeavor is made to win
that person to Christ. Cooperation among Christians often leads
to laxity toward those who know nothing of the new and abundant life.

A third theological cause of fog is defining the church's mission

---

*Robert H. Schuller, *Your Church Has Real Possibilities* (Glendale, CA: Regal
Press, 1974).

in terms of only one emphasis. The church of Jesus Christ is a big, broad Body and must not define its mission in terms of only one emphasis. Nevertheless, some congregations emphasize worship as sufficient mission; others, social service; others, renewal; and still others, Christian education. All these emphases are good and must be done, but they should never be substituted for the deliberate costly winning of the lost.

There's also a practical reason for the fog: Many Christians are engrossed solely in maintaining their local churches. Now churches need to be maintained. We need programs, administration, music, Sunday schools, and so on. All these are necessary. However, no congregation should be engaged solely or even largely in maintenance. Every church should be bringing men and women to Christ and adding them to the Body.

What is needed to remove the fog?

Members need to gather, view, and interpret the facts. Congregations need to see and understand the facts and be motivated by them. Let the congregation help in discerning the Body of Christ. Let the congregation clearly see the Body of Christ, measuring the different rates of growth, describing the different parts of the Body, and discovering why one part of the Body is growing better than another.

The facts we need are easy to obtain, and getting them is a fascinating employment. Many members are qualified to find the facts and would be delighted to have a part. In some churches, members are dealing with statistics and graphs in their secular employment. In one of our Church Growth Seminars, an intelligent woman was extremely interested in everything that was happening. I found that her profession was analyzing charts and graphs for the city planning commission; yet she hadn't used her expertise to compile facts for her own church. Her tremendous talent was waiting to be used. Many congregations have members with similar abilities.

The first fact you need is the growth history of the total field—facts about your denomination and your congregation across the years. For example, the Conservative Baptists separated from the American Baptists some years ago on doctrinal issues. The Conservative Baptists believed they were more evangelical and truer to the Scriptures. Recently, Roger Hedlund completed a doctoral dissertation on the growth patterns and potentials of the Conservative Baptists in the United States. He discovered that while the Conservative Baptists were separating from the American Baptists, they grew fantastically. Once the division was completed, they plateaued. Conservative Baptists believed themselves to be more theologically sound, more evangelical, more concerned with the lost, and more effective in proclamation; yet their growth history was a plateau. That discovery shook Dr. Hedlund, and it shook others. But the facts were clear, and once they were seen, Conservative Baptists could take remedial action. One positive result of the Church Growth movement is that people come out of the fog, discern what is happening, and begin to take remedial action.

A similar process happens at the local church level. In a Church Growth Seminar in Mesa, Arizona, leaders gathered to consider their church. Facts had been previously compiled by the pastor and members of the board. When these facts were placed on charts and graphs, the leaders experienced a resounding impact. They discovered that the community had been skyrocketing in growth; yet their church had been declining. This fact was used by the Holy Spirit to turn the church around from decline to growth, from self-centeredness to reaching the nonchurched.

Getting the facts is similar to the process a doctor follows. A doctor takes your temperature with a thermometer. A thermometer doesn't cure what you have, but it does tell something about your condition. Statistics tell something about the church's condition. Graphs give a picture that helps a church think creatively and constructively. They aid diagnosis so that a proper cure may be prescribed and an appropriate remedy applied.

The first facts needed are the large totals for a whole denomination or a whole congregation across the years. These show general trends and give the large picture; yet these totals are thin figures. We must go on to get the subtotals. Suppose at the denominational level you were to list all the congregations as follows: big, static urban churches, small struggling urban churches, big growing urban churches, big static rural churches, and small dying rural churches. Suppose you were to get those subtotals for the last twenty years. You would then have an understanding, now hidden from view, of what is happening in your denomination. Suppose you listed all the congregations in your district/ conference/presbytery/denomination in just two categories— mother churches who have produced one or more daughter churches in the last ten years; barren churches who have never had a daughter, are not now pregnant, and don't plan to have a daughter church in the future. You would have two interesting subtotals that would tell you quite a bit about the future of your churches.

You could easily secure other kinds of subtotals for your congregation: graphs of growth for various age groups, occupational profiles of members contrasted with those of the community, graphs of biological, transfer, and conversion growth.

In the past, some denominations have relied almost exclusively upon biological increase. In those days, the normal family had four, five, or six children, and all were nurtured in "the fear and admonition of the Lord." As these children of believers became Christians, denominations grew. One could reasonably expect that with only biological growth and good Christian nurture the future of a denomination would be assured.

Today we face a very different situation. This is the era of the pill. Zero population growth is the national and international goal. Families limit themselves to one or two children. Some families choose to have none. In the United States many denominations are now realizing that their membership is steadily declining and will continue to do so. A denomination which continues to rely solely or even largely on biological growth will not be here one hundred years from now. Such churches are slowly committing suicide.

Can one predict the growth or decline of a congregation or denomination?

"Yes," says Dr. Foster H. Shannon in an article in *Church Growth: America* II, no. 2 (March/April 1976), entitled "Predicting Church Growth."

The single most significant factor to determine whether a church grows or does not grow is *new members received as a per cent of membership*. The statement should be a tautology or a truism, but it is not. Frequently we hear someone say, "Our church received thirty new members" or "fifty new members" or "one hundred new members last year." Do you ever hear someone speak in terms of new members received as a percent of membership? Yet this is a far more significant factor for two reasons:

1. Growth cannot take place unless more members are received than are lost. This should be obvious!

2. Less obvious but equally true—churches will lose members by death, transfer or membership attrition.

Some churches lose far too many members. They should be concerned about the quality of their programs of fellowship and nurture—that there not be such a loss of members. Perhaps a loss of four percent by attrition is a reasonable, albeit, regrettable expectation. Churches that are losing substantially more than four percent of their total membership by attrition should especially examine the way they handle new church members.

I have made a special study of the United Presbyterian Church as a denomination, and also of selected local congregations within the United Presbyterian family. I believe that most of my observations are valid for all Protestant denominations in the United States.

In the Presbyterian Church when the three loss factors are added together (death, transfer, attrition), about eight percent of the total membership is lost each year. This is true for the denomination and for most presbyteries. It is also true for most congregations.

You can make a simple chart for your church for the past five, ten or twenty years. Make a proportional scale. With a solid line indicate number of members for each year. That line will, of course, indicate whether the total number of members has been increasing or decreasing. Now with a broken line indicate new members received as a percent of membership and place that on the chart at a one-tenth factor. That is, the same line that would indicate 100 members would also indicate ten new members received or the same line that indicated 500 members would indicate fifty new members received. Now look at the two lines on your graph. If the dotted line is either equal to or above the solid line, then future church growth is predicted. If the dotted line is more than slightly below the solid line, then membership declension is predicted. In my studies I have shown this to be true for many, many churches.

Are other factors to be considered?

As we discern the Body reverently and describe it scientifically, we dissipate the fog swirling around us. By gathering pertinent facts about the growth and development of our churches, we see what is really happening. In addition, we discover the social structures that influence the growth of the Body. Social structures of many varieties largely determine whether Church Growth occurs or not and whether or not evangelism is effective.

For example, in one year, a large Baptist denomination in the United States added one hundred twelve thousand people by baptism to its membership. Excellent growth! But one must ask, What was the social structure of those baptisms? They were not just individuals. They belonged to certain groups, certain social units. A person with Church Growth eyes asks, "How does that overall figure break down? Did eighty thousand baptisms come from within that denomination through biological growth [children of Christians growing up in that denomination]? Did twenty thousand baptisms come from children who grew up in other Baptist churches? Did ten thousand baptisms come from denominations of infant baptizers? Did two thousand baptisms come from hard-core humanists, rationalists, and Marxists?"

When the above questions were asked of a top denominational official of that church, he looked puzzled and said, "I don't know, but I'm going to find out." If he does, he will discover something of how that denomination is growing, how it has grown in the past, and how it can expect to grow in the future if it continues the same growth processes. Such facts will indicate where that denomination needs to work, pray, and invest energy in the important days ahead. This illustration applies as well to every local church as it discovers and interprets the "subtotals."

How can my congregation develop Church Growth eyes?

Let the entire congregation begin thinking about, discussing, learning the pertinent facts, teaching others, reading books, praying, and *doing something* about Church Growth.

Fortunately, many helps are available. Motivate the congregation by showing films, such as those listed in Appendix A. Right after they see the film, enroll leaders of the church in a class to study Church Growth. Get them to discuss books about Church Growth and work their way through, chapter by chapter, asking, How does that apply to us? Do we have that kind of situation? Use resources (Appendix A) and complete the worksheets in Appendix B, which are helpful in discerning the Body. After the group has discussed issues raised in this book, they will develop abiding convictions about the possibilities of Church Growth in their particular environment.

You can have a significant part in helping others in your church dissipate the fog. Help them get the facts and discuss Church Growth. Encourage them to pray about Church Growth. Lead them to do something about the growth of Christ's church. Remember, a right understanding of the Body of Christ, discerned reverently and described accurately and scientifically, assists Christian leaders in being good stewards of the grace of God and effective communicators of the gospel of Christ.

QUESTIONS FOR REVIEW AND DISCUSSION

1. What are the advantages for a church to discern the body?
2. An analogy of the Body of Christ and the human body has many implications. Discuss them.

3. In cases where a church is not growing, discerning the Body can be a difficult and soul-searching experience. What attitudes on the part of the church members, board, and pastor would facilitate a proper perspective toward this activity?
4. Are there any types of "fog" existing presently in your church? Discuss them and what methods would be appropriate for removing them.
5. What facts would be particularly interesting and relevant to your church? How would you go about securing them?
6. Make a general comparative graph between the growth of your church in the last ten years and the growth of your community. What are the trends and the future at the rate?
7. Reread the section by Dr. Foster Shannon on "predicting growth." Then create a graph with your own figures. Discuss the implications.

6

Churches Grow As They Rightly Discern the Community

The community is the environment in which the Body lives. Churches grow as they rightly discern the community.

How do I go about discerning my community?

Community has typically been defined in terms of geography, that is, people who live within certain areas. However, for Church Growth thinking, it is more useful to define *community* as a group sharing common characteristics and/or interests. In a given geographical area many different kinds of people can exist. An adequate understanding of *community* seeks to identify and understand the various groupings and the ways in which they interact.

For a congregation to rightly discern its community, it must begin by identifying its ministry area—the territory within a reasonable driving distance of the church. This distance will vary in different parts of the country. For example, in Southern California the reasonable driving distance is twenty to twenty-five minutes; in Seattle, Washington, fifteen to twenty minutes. In western Kansas, with its wide, open plains, people will drive forty-five minutes. However, the rising cost of fuel is changing how much people are willing and able to use their cars. In the near future (and already in some parts of the country) churches will have to consider carefully the availability of public transportation and, in its absence, the problems created by inflation and the energy crunch.

A simple way to determine the ministry area is to mark on a map the location of the church. Place other pins to indicate homes of members. The area within the pins is that from which the church draws its membership. Using the church as the center, draw a circle which represents a reasonable commuting distance. Within that circle is the church's primary ministry area. Such a circle will include not only present, active members but often thousands of unchurched people.

Identifying the ministry area is a liberating experience for pastor and people. The boundaries of their ministry area are not halfway between their church and the next but a reasonable commuting distance from the church. Nor should pastor and people feel intimidated by other churches in their ministry area.

The next step is to identify communities within the ministry area. These can be differentiated in several ways, for example, by kinds of houses. One part of the community may live in one-hundred-thousand-dollar houses. Another, in twenty-thousand-dollar homes. These people don't have much in common even if they all speak English. They have different values, ways of spending their leisure time, occupations, expectations from life, and expectations from the church.

There will probably be blue-collar workers and white-collar workers. There are university and nonuniversity sections. There is the church crowd and the nonchurch crowd. Each group can be easily identified on any warm, summer Sunday morning by driving down a residential street.

The ministry area may include diverse ethnic and linguistic groupings. At least fifty-eight million people in the United States consider themselves ethnics. Their rising sense of heritage and tradition has enhanced the advisability of establishing ethnic churches. This is not "un-Christian." In fact, it may be un-Christian to demand that the ethnic become part of a white, middle-class congregation. In the United States, the melting pot hasn't been very hot. Racial, color, language, and cultural distinctions are important considerations for the growth of the church.

In addition to these overall distinctions, there are subdistinctions. For example, most white people think the Blacks are one community. Nothing could be further from the truth. There are many kinds of Blacks—highly educated, wealthy, poor, uneducated, farm workers, surgeons, educators, and so on. The same distinctions apply equally to white communities. Certain congregations will be more effective in reaching certain kinds of people. Since all people need to be evangelized, effective Church Growth strategy recognizes the diversities within a given ministry area and focuses its message for responsiveness.

In great measure, responsiveness is related to approach. The good fisherman will take along a variety of bait. If the fish are not responding to worms, he will switch to flies, and one kind of fly will be more effective in certain seasons than others. The good fisherman continues to seek responsiveness until he discovers the right bait for a particular fish during a particular season. He knows when he has the right bait—he's catching fish!

As fish respond to one approach and not to another, so do people. This is the truth behind the common opinion that a friendly church is a growing church. It is a matter of response. If a church is friendly, genuinely interested in people, and meeting their needs, it will find people responsive. They will be open to the Good News. On the other hand, if a church is cold and reserved, that church will probably find people in its ministry area cold and indifferent. Each church, much like the fisherman, seeks responsiveness by using the right approach at the right time. In so doing, churches will be effective and obedient to Christ's command to be fishers of men.

Are you saying that my responsibility is only to people like me? What about the rest of the people in my ministry area?

While people with similar life-styles and backgrounds are a primary target for near-neighbor evangelism, there is a second responsibility toward people one step removed by occupation, income, language, culture. These people are winnable by E-2 evangelism. Sometimes they can be won into our congregations. Sometimes they can be won into branch churches which will occasionally worship with our congregation. Sometimes they can be won only to congregations of people who worship in their own language.

Good strategy is for each church to have a task force of Christians consciously engaged in stepping across cultural barriers. This task force, if located in a church in Southern California, should be learning Spanish and planning to start a Spanish-speaking church. This principle could be applied in many cities with many languages. Why shouldn't congregations all over North America have 5 percent of their members learning another culture and its language and starting churches among the un-churched multitudes of that culture?

There is New Testament precedent for the Church finding ways to step over culture barriers. For fifteen to twenty years, the New Testament church spoke the Word only to Jews. It was a _Jewish_ church. Initially, the church didn't believe it could or should evangelize Gentiles. For many years the apostles confined their message to the Jews. Then some laymen in Antioch spoke to the Greeks about Jesus, won them to the Lord, baptized them, and started Gentile congregations. The church had crossed the culture barrier. It took a deliberate act of the Holy Spirit to thrust the church forward. Today the Holy Spirit yearns to find laymen willing to cross culture barriers. He has urgent work for them to do in nearby "Gentile" territory.

Are you advocating segregation?

No. Segregation means keeping people out. That is certainly not the function of the church. The church of Jesus Christ is one, intentionally and constitutionally. If it isn't _one_, it isn't the church. However, from the very beginning there has been plenty of room for diversity within oneness.

Look around at your next denominational meeting. Do the representatives from individual churches really represent the many diverse groups of people who should be served by that denomination? If so, you will find a sensitive and obedient denomination. If the people all look the same, perhaps your denomination needs to break out to Puerto Ricans, Filipinos, Chinese, Arabs, French, Blacks, and others. A denomination with congregations in many various population groupings is alive and alert to the real situation in America today.

Growing congregations are usually composed primarily of like people. Others, of course, are cordially welcome, but the church made up of different kinds of people about equally distributed is generally a nongrowing church. True, in some cities there are churches composed of people from many different nationalities, but most of these congregations are heavily subsidized by the denomination because they don't grow and don't multiply themselves.

Barriers, and often hostility, certainly exist between segments of society. Christians should work toward removing these barriers and diminishing hostility. The best way to do this is to seed all segments of society with living churches. While we work toward unity and hold this as the ideal, growth-oriented churches accept the fact that a certain amount of likeness among the members aids the spread of the gospel.

How and where does one secure information for rightly discerning the community?

Knowledge of a community can readily be obtained. Schools, for example, are an excellent indicator. The boys and girls attending a school are fairly representative of the families in that area. The city planning department has a good knowledge of community make-up. High-school and college sociology teachers are an excellent source. A task force of vigorous Christians could analyze the area, construct a large map, and identify the groupings. In so doing, the would find great opportunities for planting churches. A church planter in Cincinnati, Ohio, recently discovered such an opportunity. In his endeavor to find responsive and neglected segments of the community, he discovered that executives living in one-hundred-thousand-dollar homes were one of the unreached groups of that city. He had found a responsive unit and is now seeing significant results.

By rightly discerning the community, needs and opportunities for growth will surface.

QUESTIONS FOR REVIEW AND DISCUSSION

1. Discuss the concept of *community* as defined by the authors. How does this idea affect your church's outreach thinking instead of community defined geographically?
2. Determine your ministry area. Draw this on a map and discuss its implications.
3. Divide your ministry area into separate communities. What areas would be most responsive to your church and its people?
4. Make a list of all the possible means and sources available to begin discerning your community.

7

Churches Grow As They Find New Groups and Ways to Disciple

Pentecost was a red-letter day in the growth of the church: Believers increased from 120 to 3120! For some time after Pentecost, the church grew explosively among the Jews. Then a small overflow occurred among Samaritans who were half-Jews. A small band of Romans soon became followers of Jesus. Believers were still, however, largely from among the common Jewish people. The Pharisees, Sadducees, upper classes, rulers, King Herod, and King Agrippa did not become Christians.

The early church—until about A.D. 46—"made disciples" in obedience to its Lord. It marched under the banner of the Great Commission, reaching out in effective evangelism, but it multiplied congregations only among the Jews. Then some laymen of Cyprus and Cyrene, on coming to Antioch, forgot that they ought to speak the Word to the Jews only, and spoke to the Greeks also. They must have been vividly conscious of the command of Christ and had a high degree of commitment.

Like the early church, churches throughout history have grown strong in one segment of society and then, under the impact of Christ's command, carried the Gospel across a race, culture, or language barrier. The process can be seen again and again.

Churches began in one segment of the population, flourished, and then spread. *Churches and denominations grow as they find new segments of the population and disciple them.*

Does this principle function today?

For many decades the Swedish Baptists in North America grew chiefly among Swedes. They were an ethnic church. Then in the late 1930s there was a movement of the Holy Spirit, and the Swedes saw a new vision of what Christ wanted them to do. They realized they were living in the midst of multitudes of unreached people who were not Swedish Americans. They resolved to cease concentrating on Americans of Swedish background and to win Americans of all backgrounds. They decided to call themselves the Baptist General Conference, and they have grown from forty thousand in 1940 to over one hundred thousand in 1976. This group projects that its number will double again in the next decade.

The Covenant denomination also began among Swedes. It grew rapidly as long as Swedes immigrated to this country, but when immigration stopped, so did significant growth. Today Covenant churches are struggling to break out of their ethnicity. Yet this must happen if they are to flourish and be obedient to Christ's Great Commission. The sense of obedience must be intense, for any denomination naturally wants to hold to and respect its heritage. Yet it must deliberately add to its fellowship persons of diverse backgrounds, or growth will be stifled.

For four hundred years the Mennonites have maintained a flame of Christian devotion. Under severe persecution in Switzerland, Holland, Prussia, and Russia, they left rather than compromise. It is a wonderful denomination; but for four hundred years it has been made up of "born Mennonites." Mennonites have evangelized existing, cold, lapsed, or nominal Mennonites. When evangelized, these people became warm, believing Mennonites. Now Mennonites are realizing that in addition to being a good ethnic church they must be a good general church. Perhaps they will break the barriers to add to their redemptive fellowship large numbers of the unsaved from other ethnic backgrounds. Lost people are all around them in North America. Spanish-speaking Mennonite churches? Black Mennonite churches? Irish Mennonite churches? Why not?

Are you suggesting that by studying how denominations and local churches started we can find important clues as to how a denomination might keep itself growing and reach out to all people?

Indeed! We spoke earlier of the Conservative Baptist denomination which formed itself almost entirely out of existing Northern Baptists. Baptists who were firm in their faith, believed in the infallible authority of Scripture, were evangelical and more definite in their beliefs than the general run of Baptists became Conservative Baptists. However, once that division was completed, once that particular segment of the Christian population had been won, the Conservative Baptist denomination plateaued. To grow, it must now find effective means to evangelize non-Christians.

Another illustration of the need to "bridge" is seen among the Friends—a fine denomination that originated in England. Pacifism, love and help of fellow man, rigorous self-discipline, and inner light characterized the Societies of Friends started among weavers and the ordinary people of England. Those who join the Friends *now* are not, by and large, the common people. They are not weavers and factory laborers. They are not new immigrants. Today, Friends are middle-class or upper-middle-class white Americans. The Friends have to find ways to disciple Americans who do not belong to this segment of society. They have discipled "the Jews," now they have to find ways to disciple the "Gentiles." It may be that some of their laymen on coming to Antioch will speak to the Greeks also, telling them of the Lord Jesus, and they will begin to found "Greek" Friends Churches. That would be wonderful!

Holding to one's past, yet wanting to break from it, poses quite a problem.

The Christian Reformed Church and the Reformed Church in American, with their Dutch background and strong Calvinistic faith, find it difficult to incorporate people of other homogeneous units. In conversation with a pastor of one of these denominations, I asked, "If a Christian of Irish or Italian background joined one of your churches, proving to be a faithful member, how long would it be before he might be elected to an office or place of leadership?" After considering that question a few moments, the pastor said, "He should plan on twelve to fifteen years!"

The Reformed Presbyterian and the Orthodox Presbyterian Churches didn't begin by taking in publicans and sinners. They took in the very best Presbyterians they could, the soundest in the faith, and withdrew into a different denomination. Today, I imagine their problem is to find ways of contacting unsaved and unsound men and women and incorporating *them* in their very sound congregations.

The Christian and Missionary Alliance in America grew from the cream of the crop. Christians from several churches formed a "missionary society" to take the Good News to the world. Welded together by this enthralling task, they established their own denomination. They too now face a problem. Until recently, they have for the most part been adding to their churches a few Christian people who had great missionary passion. Such people, plus the biological increase, provided the Christian and Missionary Alliance with limited growth in America. Many of their leaders now recognize that they must build bridges to factory laborers, Chicanos, and others who haven't been within the scope of their ministry.

Some congregations and denominations get "stuck" because they are such "good" Christians that they isolate themselves from outsiders. That is not to say that the church should lower standards in order to win people. Rather, the Christian must multiply contact with the world while remaining separate and holy. Christians must not be so separated and so holy that they flinch every time they see a sinner. They must establish cordial, friendly, and genuine relationships. This is where new converts shine. As they meet non-Christians, without trying, they say to themselves, "I was like you myself." New converts have many contacts in "the world." These contacts comprise a great reservoir of non-Christians to whom the new converts can witness. They are findable sheep!

The Christian is in the world yet not of the world. It is very difficult to love the people in the world and yet hate the world. That is the problem every Christian faces if effective evangelism is to take place. Christians and churches must find ways to be in but not of the world.

How then do you find ways to keep a church growing?

First, we have to overcome the "choke law." That law was stated by a missionary in Tanzania. He observed that as a church grows the existing members tend to absorb the entire time, attention, and budget of both laymen and pastors. "Maintenance" chokes off evangelistic outreach, and growth stops.

There is always plenty to do in existing congregations and denominations. Deacons, elders, and pastors are inclined to spend their entire time and affections caring for what they already have. It is common to see a church with two, three, or more pastors all carrying on maintenance, but the church shows no growth. Such a church has succumbed to the "choke law."

This law operates on the mission field where forty, fifty, or more missionaries serve perhaps a hundred congregations. They are all doing "good church and mission work," but the church is not growing. Many laymen today work at looking after the existing church. They work at making the church better by visiting, serving, educating, and edifying members, but the church remains about the same size. This is the "choke law" in operation.

Overcoming this law begins with measuring church growth.

Measurement enables each congregation to monitor its own state of health. If it is not growing, something is wrong. If the growth line on the graph does not go up, something must be done. We need to break into new segments of the population. We need to be more obedient to the Great Commission. We need to discover and implement ways to reach the lost.

Entire denominations have ceased growing, and this should be of great concern to their leaders. In most cases, nongrowth will continue until concerned Christians assign substantial amounts of time, money, and prayer directly to growth.

When a congregation or denomination has plateaued, how can it get moving?

That is a key question. Perhaps it can be answered through an illustration.

While conducting a series of Church Growth Seminars in Houston, Texas, Dr. Arn had an afternoon free to visit the Johnson Space Center where communication and control is carried on between earth and orbiting satellites. This futuristic, technological center was an impressive sight. The control room, with its banks of television monitors, illuminated maps for tracking satellites, and communication network was mind boggling. In one corner of the room was a flag back from the moon; in another corner, moon rocks.

His greatest thrill that afternoon was to stand at the base of one of the rockets which pointed heavenward and realize that its bulk is made up of engines and fuel necessary to lift it off the launch pad and break it free of gravity. Most Americans have seen a rocket launch on television. The count down hits zero, the gantry falls away, "ignition" is called, smoke belches out, fire and roar, then very slowly, the rocket lifts from the pad and heads toward space. Enormous power is needed to start it on its way. Once that rocket is in outer space, however, little power is required to keep it moving and on course. The most difficult part of a space launch is moving that mass off the pad and heading it in the right direction.

There is a parallel in Church Growth. When a church or denomination has plateaued or is declining, all available thrust is necessary—prayer, time, concentrated effort, appropriation of dollars—to get it off the launch pad and moving into growth. Once moving, however, once it has built in growth principles, comparatively small efforts are necessary to keep it growing. The basic problem is to employ all available resources in overcoming inertia, gravity, and indifference and lifting that church the first hundred feet toward growth and outreach. At this point many churches fall crashing back to earth. They do not purpose to put in the energy, prayer, finances, and manpower necessary for growth. They do not intend to get their static church actually evangelizing new and unchurched elements of the population. They do not pray fervently to God for power to bring penitent sinners into their fellowship. They do not make visitors feel at home.

Congregations often develop mechanisms which unintentionally exclude new members. Churches need to look at themselves carefully at this point. For example, Mr. X comes through the front door as a new member. He is given the right hand of fellowship. He is told he is loved. He is given offering envelopes. Mr. X then begins looking for a group with whom he can identify and be a part.

I was once an X. I had received the right hand of fellowship along with the offering envelopes. I had been told how much I was loved and how happy I would be in the church. However, I soon discovered that groups of people who knew each other spent most of their time within those groups. People all seemed to "belong." I didn't! Perhaps the problem was with me. I tried a few groups, and they were "friendly" but did not incorporate me. Eventually, I did what every other X does. I drifted out the back door. We don't speak much of the back door, but evangelism is ineffective if the front door and the back door are both wide open. The back door will remain open unless smaller groups within the larger Body not only "welcome" new people but really incorporate them into the fellowship.

The same love and caring that brings people into any church must be exercised by groups within that church so that newcomers really become "one of us." The new person has to be "grafted" into some group in the church, and that takes doing.

You mentioned previously that the "right mix" keeps a church growing.

Many ingredients go into the "mix," and the proportion is important. One ingredient is "the kind of people we are." We easily attract that kind of people.

For example, a youth ministry featuring basketball will bring in just one ingredient—boys who love basketball. A bus ministry will also appeal to, and consciously enlist, only people of a certain social stratum.

One ingredient of the right mix, then, is the kind of people. Other ingredients include the charisma of the minister, the fervency of the message, successfully incorporating new converts, and utilizing lay leadership. No one ingredient is *the* way. The *mix* is the important thing. We must find the right proportion of ingredients, and different mixes will be necessary for different congregations and different churches in different areas. Fervency, biblical soundness, friendliness, speaking to the "Greeks," incorporating in new congregations kinds of people not now in the congregation. Churches grow and continue to grow as they find the right proportion of ingredients.

How do you know when you have the right mix?

When the church is growing, you have the right mix! If the church is not growing, you had better keep adding new methods, new convictions, and stirring. A smooth-running motor has the right mixture of gas and air flowing into the cylinders. If it is backfiring, you have the wrong mix. If a church is not growing, keep adjusting the ingredients—more of this, less of that. When the church starts growing, you have the right mix.

As a car gains speed, the mixture of gas and oxygen must keep changing. Once you have found the right mix, keep using it, but keep measuring its effectiveness. The same old mix won't work forever. In a rapidly changing age, where conditions differ, neighborhoods fluctuate, and society is extremely mobile, the mix for Church Growth needs constant attention.

Some Christians believe they have found the right mix when their evangelism brings a person to make a "decision." The right mix, however, should bring converts into the church of the person who is witnessing. When evangelism seems to win people to Christ and yet doesn't incorporate them into the witness's own church, evangelism is incomplete.

The aim of evangelism is that men and women become disciples and responsible members of Christ's church. Ingredients should be juggled until people are joining *your* church. That is the goal. It is difficult, almost impossible, to win people into somebody else's church. The only church you can effectively win people into is your own. If you think that after you "win them to Christ" they will find a church that suits them, you are badly mistaken. If, after you lead them to Christ, you suggest they join someone else's church, you will see them join *none*. The only church you can effectively win people to is your own. Failure to remember this will frequently render evangelism ineffective. Evangelism that doesn't add people to the Body is not the right mix. Unless those who make "decisions for Christ" become active disciples, responsible members of the church, their decision usually fades rapidly into oblivion.

I've been looking for right methods in all of this. So far, no luck.

There is no doubt that some methods add to the growth of the church. God has used many methods. We have only to look around us to see many successful methods, but a congregation generally makes a mistake when it takes a "method" someone else has used and merely copies it. A congregation does much better to develop its own sense of urgency in finding people and, from that sense of urgency and conviction, find the methods that work. They will be the right methods.

There are hundreds of ways to grow. The creative congregation will find these ways. Sometimes they will be methods that have been used for a thousand years; sometimes they will be ways no one has ever before used. Hundreds of creative means are yet to be found and are but one idea away.

For instance, a group of "young marrieds" attended a Church Growth Seminar. They became deeply concerned that other young adults be reached for Christ. How? They struggled with the question until a creative answer was found. They were fans of professional football; so they asked, "How can we use this interest to reach other young adults for Christ?" The idea! A series of season tickets for the home games was purchased and used to take along non-Christian friends. In one season, they not only enjoyed the games but had the immense pleasure of winning nine young couples to Christ and to their church.

But what happens when everything you try fails?

There will be failures, no doubt about it. But we must fall back on the Lord's statement that our Father works, the Lord Jesus works, and we have to work. Much hard work goes into the growth of a church. Read Paul's account of his labors, shipwrecks, beatings, hungers, and thirstings and realize the tremendous effort he put forward. Effort is an essential ingredient. When our church or denomination is not growing, we are called to exert Herculean efforts, confident that as we do so God will grant us strength and power.

Church Growth takes work. Converts are not picked up as we stroll casually down the beach. Our faith has to be white hot before it will ignite faith in others. The future will not automatically happen by merely wishing hard enough. Growth requires decision—now! Growth imposes risks—now! Growth requires action—now! Growth demands allocation of resources—now! Growth requires work—now. When this happens, God gives the increase!

Growth is not automatic. There is strain, labor, travail, pain, and anguish. In the growth of a church there is as much stress as in the birth and growth of a child.

There is a paradox in growth. If a church wants to be more effective tomorrow in finding the lost, it must start acting like a more-effective church today. A church of thirty-five needs to begin thinking, acting, witnessing, and serving like a church of a hundred. The church of a hundred needs to begin thinking and acting like the church of two hundred. A congregation that wants to grow has to support key activities on the level needed after growth has taken place. At the same time, however, such a church does not usually have the resources. Only by "starving" all but the truly essential components can a congregation fight off conflicting requirements of the present and still create the church of tomorrow. The Lord Jesus talks of pruning; that which does not bear fruit is cut away. Churches will grow when they cut off activities that do not find the lost and increase activities that *do*. Activities that do not advance the gospel not only drain but also impede growth potential.

Your assumption seems to be that a church can and should keep growing. Do you believe this?

The church of Jesus Christ must grow continually. Unchurched mllions remain to be won.

One of the disastrous myths with which many Christians quiet their uneasy consciences is that they are living in a fairly well-churched country. Many really believe Satan's big lie: All who can be won, have been won.

A Methodist minister of a church of forty-seven members, in a generally Catholic town, once said to me with a wry smile, "I used to believe we had won everyone in this town who could be won. Then the Assemblies of God came along. They hadn't heard that all the winnable had been won, and within three years they had a church of over two hundred members."

Would you say God may cast aside a congregation that is not growing and send in a new one?

If the old one is no longer obedient, no longer doing the job and finding the lost, beyond question, God will send in a new one! Lutherans, Methodists, Assemblies of God, and others have been *sent* by God. I am not so sure, however, that God casts the old one aside. If he does, he casts it aside temporarily as he did Israel, as recorded in Romans 11:16–20. A temporary insensitivity has come upon Israel until the full number of Gentiles have been admitted. Then, as Paul said, Israel will come back in.

Churches and denominations that have plateaued and are now going downhill must pray and seek a fresh infusion of the Holy Spirit. When this comes, they will surge forward in joyful obedience. May God grant to dormant congregations and denominations a fresh vision for the lostness of men to the end that the lost be found and his just and holy name be known in more and more sections of the vast mosaic of mankind.

QUESTIONS FOR REVIEW AND DISCUSSION

1. What new segments of your ministry area could be reached by your church? What new approaches would be required?
2. Are there barriers your church has inadvertently created that limit its growth in its ministry area? Identify and suggest ways these may be removed.
3. Is the "choke law" functioning at all in your church?
4. How can your church increase the feeling of belonging of new converts like Mr. X?
5. How can failure contribute to church growth?
6. Take a look at the evangelistic "mix" of your church. Do the ingredients need changing? Do the proportions need adjusting?

8

Churches Grow As They Reproduce Themselves Through Planned Parenthood

When you speak of planned parenthood, you certainly don't mean limiting growth. What do you mean?

Churches grow by expansion, that is, by present congregations growing larger. They also grow by deliberately planting new churches—planned parenthood. Church planting needs to be taken seriously because the need for new churches is enormous.

Almost every community in America appears to be well churched. Because church buildings have existed for years and their doors have always been open to anyone who wants to attend, one tends to conclude that more churches are not needed. This is wrong because while some people appear to have enough churches, enormous numbers of people are unchurched and will remain so if only present-day churches exist.

For example, in West Virginia, 60 percent of the population does not confess Jesus Christ. West Virginia has 1,800,800 people. Since 60 percent do not profess belief in Jesus Christ, 1,080,000 people are unchurched. West Virginia has enormous numbers of people who should be in Christ and in the church. Most of these lost people will not join an existing congregation near their homes because of some income, ethnic, linguistic, or geographic reason. They need new congregations or subcongregations. The church must press out into every segment of society by fellowships, Christian cells, and new churches until a much larger proportion of the American people confess faith in Christ, become disciples, and live as responsible members of his church.

When you talk about planting new churches, aren't you really talking about interchurch competition? We have enough competition between churches and denominations.

That objection is well answered by Wendell Belew of the Southern Baptist Home Mission Department in an article appearing in *Church Growth: America.* He states:

"Two churches are more complementary than competitive. Two churches minister to people of two different mind sets, two different cultural inclinations. They will reach nearly twice as many unchurched as one will. We need not be afraid of competition between denominations or local churches. I really do not know of any situation anywhere where one church "devoured" another by over-growing it, unless one of the churches had ceased to witness and had determined not to grow."

Birth and growth are the rhythm of life as are living and dying. People move away. Communities change. Churches grow old and die. We must constantly be planting new churches.

We do not advocate rushing out wild-eyed and starting churches everywhere without planning, expertise, or know-how. We advocate using the best information and minds available, the best intuition we have. Our community is our mission field, and we should establish churches in it with the same creative intelligence and dedication we expect of missionaries.

George Patterson, Baptist missionary in Honduras, thinks creatively about new churches. He uses the analogy of links in a chain. Every link should be a church-planting link. Unfortunately, some churches become "dead-end links." They may function as a church but they do not connect with links—they do not reproduce.

Every church ought to say to itself, "We owe our birth to somebody else. Are we going to be a dead-end link? Does the process of church planting end with us, or are we going to confer on some other community, some other group of people, the privilege of knowing Jesus Christ?" The opportunity may not be to establish a church on the next block, but you won't have to go many blocks or miles before you find great opportunities to extend the chain.

Here's a possibility. Let every church have a task force of maybe 2 percent of its members who deliberately learn another culture, perhaps another language, perhaps another life-style, and then serve as "midwives" in planting new congregations. We need tens of thousands of home missionaries, volunteers, who earn their living as teachers, executives, administrators, taxi drivers, or farmers but give a regular portion of their time to planting new Christian cells in some neglected segment of the population.

A man who drove a bus for a county school system in Canada was delivering eight or ten children out into the hills to a small community. None of the people went to church anywhere. In fact, the people had no church to go to unless they drove fifteen miles. The bus driver determined to establish a Christian cell among those families. Because there were only thirteen homes, the fellowship would probably be more a chapel than a church, but if he hadn't planted a Christian cell, those people would have continued to be out of contact with Christ and would have remained unbelievers. To let clusters of people remain without conscious dedication to Christ is sin and must not be tolerated.

In South Korea in a district called Soon Chun, Pastor Ahn, a Korean minister, and Hugh Linton, an American missionary, teamed up to establish a church within walking distance of every man, woman, and child in the province. On a huge map they put a red dot for every existing church and a blue dot for every village where there should be a church. When they started in 1965, the map was covered with blue dots. They set to work to turn those blue dots into red ones. By 1975 the goal was reached. The map was covered with red dots, churches within walking distance of every person who lived in a district. That could be done in many cities of the United States. Of course, it wouldn't be walking distance or driving distance. It would be better to say, a church within cultural distance. There should be no unchurched segments in any community or any culture.

Even churches with cultural similarities are often quite distinct. Yorba Linda Friends Church in Southern California has expanded rapidly in a growing area, however, its leaders were not satisfied to grow only by expansion. A few years ago they planted a Friends church only two miles away. Both churches are growing rapidly!

How do you account for churches of the same denomination, located in close proximity, growing so rapidly?

Dr. Charles Mylander asked the same question. He studied the two Friends churches in Southern California and found that even though they were of the same denomination in the same general geographic area they ministered to somewhat different kinds of people. Some people felt more comfortable in one church than the other, depending on their economic, social, cultural backgrounds, and their personal preferences in worship and study. The two churches are not competitive but supportive. They offer two excellent options to the people of Yorba Linda.

Different interests and needs occur from generation to generation. In a Church Growth Seminar in Canada we found that among Mennonites 37 percent of the marriages of the young people in one congregation had taken place with non-Mennonites and the couples had thereupon left the Mennonite Church. That congregation might very well consider starting a community (Mennonite) church in which these couples would feel welcome.

It seems to me that with more resources an already established church would grow faster than a new church with limited resources.

Just the opposite is true! The Nazarenes did a study of growth from 1906 to 1971. They found that in the beginning (when they had limited resources) they grew rapidly, but toward the end of that period (when they had many large wealthy congregations) they practically plateaued. They asked themselves, "How many new churches were planted per decade?" They found a close correlation between the number of churches planted and the growth of the denomination. Growth in existing churches and growth by planting new churches are both valid forms, but it seems that great growth of a denomination seldom comes by growth in existing churches. It comes by planting new congregations.

I suppose you're saying that planting churches is the New Testament way.

Every Protestant church likes to believe it is a New Testament church and does things in the biblical way, but is it really a New Testament church if it isn't planting churches?

Being a real New Testament church means believing and doing what the New Testament church did. It means planting churches as the New Testament church did. The New Testament Church was tremendously concerned with, engaged in, and *successful at* establishing new congregations. Churches were planted in Jerusalem, Judea, and Samaria. Christian churches were formed in many villages on the Samarian hills. Churches sprang up in Galilee, in Antioch, in city after city, and all around the Mediterranean. Toward the end of his life, Paul was heading toward Spain to begin planting churches there. Church multiplication was an essential part of New Testament life.

Today, in a world where three out of four persons have yet to believe in Jesus Christ and at least two out of every four have yet to *hear* of Jesus Christ, if a congregation is not reproducing, it is not a New Testament church, no matter what it calls itself!

How big should a church be before it has a daughter church?

That depends entirely on circumstances. However, any congregation that has its own building and pastor should consider having a daughter. The need is too pressing and the opportunity too great for a church to selfishly consider its own welfare and forget the unchurched multitudes.

This is the New Testament pattern. The church at Antioch established new churches on Cyprus and Asia Minor before it had a church building of its own. It didn't send "green" missionaries either. It sent its two best preachers—Paul and Barnabas. More American churches should follow that pattern.

The pattern of sending the senior pastor to establish a church? Do you really mean that?

What might happen in America if gifted pastors were freed from their comfortable pulpits and loaned to plant new churches? The Holy Spirit called Paul and Barnabas. Perhaps the Holy Spirit is calling a great number of our most able pastors and seminary professors today. In 1900, Mark Matthew accepted the call to First Presbyterian Church of Seattle with the distinct understanding that he and the church would plant churches in Seattle. Backed by the First Presbyterian Church, one by one, thirty-seven other Presbyterian churches were formed in and around Seattle. That dynamic mentality, that understanding of human need, needs to capture more ministers and more church boards and sessions.

How does a church prepare for church planting?

Church planting begins with the conviction that it is God's will that his church grow. This conviction grows into an acute consciousness of the lostness of people without Christ. When these convictions permeate the people of God, planting new congregations becomes more possible.

A congregation and denomination ought to establish the

machinery for creating new churches. Conviction needs to be incarnated in organization. There should be a permanent committee in every congregation whose duty it is to plant new churches. This committee explores the community for new-church locations. It looks for opportunities, and once it has found them sets to work creating new fellowships, chapels, and, finally, fully constituted churches.

What might be a job description for the new-church committee?

An early part of the job would be to establish the need for new churches. Survey the community, look at areas that are unchurched, find ethnic units that are not too distant, make contacts with leaders in these units, and establish the need.

A second part of the job description would be to locate a suitable meeting place. Many places can be used. Don't think only of normal church buildings. A small group of believers could meet in a motel, a storefront, or a large home. There are all kinds of possibilities.

A third task would be to cultivate the field. The church might begin by holding a vacation Bible school in that area. It might conduct a survey or establish home Bible studies.

A fourth part of the job description for the new-church committee might be to prepare the sponsoring church. Its members have to be well prepared and well informed as progress continues. The sponsoring church is like a loving parent. It needs to guide without dominating. It needs to be supportive of its new offspring yet allow it room to grow.

But a community can be overchurched, can't it?

Yes, if a community is truly *totally* churched and *all* people are truly yielded to the Lord Jesus Christ, the churches then would indeed have to ask, Should we plant a church here? But where do you find such an ideal community?

Dr. Arn was invited to a Midwestern town to conduct a series of seminars. He met with the ministers of that town who in effect said, "Win, you are welcome here. We extend Christian hospitality to you, but you need to know that we have done a thorough job of evangelizing this community. Our churches are seventy-five to one hundred years old. We have reached all those in our community who do not know Christ. If there are a few 'strays,' our doors are open. They can come. We have been here a long time."

Dr. Arn accepted the challenge. From that meeting, he went to his motel and began calling every church in the community. He asked the capacity of its sanctuary and added all the figures. Then he called the community center, the Chamber of Commerce, the telephone company, and the water company. He secured accurate figures on the number of people in that community. He found that if those churches were filled to capacity three times every Sunday morning they would have reached only one-quarter of the people in that ministry area. Similar situations can be found in most communities.

But new churches are always so small and struggling.

Churches start small, but they have to. There is a certain dimension of adventure and enthusiasm, of being a pioneer in a new world, that is a fantastic moving force in a new church. And new babies eventually grow.

In this connection, two cities in Christian Church Disciples of Christ history are worth reviewing. At the turn of the century Indianapolis had four big well-to-do Christian churches. They appointed a city missionary who planted daughter churches— small, struggling, somewhat disreputable congregations—all over Indianapolis. They met in schools, barns, homes, and storefronts. For a number of years these churches remained rather poor illustrations of what a church can be; yet today Indianapolis has fifty-seven large Christian churches. All of them own fine properties. All are reputable congregations.

In contrast, the Woodward Avenue Christian Church of Detroit believed that one Christian church in the city was enough. It grew to be a large church of four thousand members. The preacher was nationally known, a pulpiteer of great power and eloquence. When people went to Detroit, they went to Wood- ward Avenue Christian Church. The denomination was proud of its great church. But Detroit didn't have another Disciples con- gregation until 1956 because the policy was: "One strong church of our sort in Detroit is enough. We are not going to start weak new churches."

Christian Church people from Kentucky, Tennessee, Indiana, and Ohio were flooding into Detroit to get jobs in the expanding auto industry, but they didn't join Christian churches. Few of them went to Woodward Avenue. Some became Baptists, Pres- byterians, Methodists, or Lutherans. Many dropped away and were lost to the world.

If the people of North America are going to be reached for Christ, we must have growth of existing churches and multiplica- tion of new churches.

The fulfillment of the Great Commission in America will re- ceive a great impetus as existing congregations, denominations, districts, and conferences reach out with a growth conscience and establish new churches. What might happen if every group that studies this chapter would say, "Let's appoint a New Church Committee . . . Let's survey our area for needs . . . Let's observe where boys and girls are growing up without Christ and their parents are trying to live without feeding on the Bread of Heaven . . . Let's believe that God wants us to start a new cell of His Body."

That is planned parenthood. One every nine months!

QUESTIONS FOR REVIEW AND DISCUSSION

1. Discuss how your church originally came into being. What dream did the early founders have? What were their reasons for planting and their expectations for growth?

2. Discuss the statement "If a congregation is not reproducing, it is not a New Testament Church."
3. Suppose your church were going to plant a new church. How would you go about it?
4. Would planting a church be a realistic, achievable goal for your church? What are the facts?

9

Churches Grow As They Structure for Growth

Are there practical helps and suggestions to enable my church to grow?

Yes. The following ten steps have been used effectively. These are practical suggestions that should be considered by every church that wants growth.

I. BUILD A CONSCIENCE CONCERNING GROWTH.

Growth conscience is a conviction that permeates the Body of Christ that God's will is for growth, that a church has the opportunity, privilege, and responsibility to carry out God's will regarding those who have yet to believe, and that programs and activities should serve this end.

A growth conscience helps overcome the static pattern built into many churches. When members constantly look back over the past ten or fifteen years, they perpetuate static thinking.

The church not actively finding the lost is only a partial church. Indeed, accepting ingrownness of the church as if it were God's will may be the chief heresy of the latter part of the twentieth century. People often think the church can be the church whether it grows or not. When shepherds stay in the sheepfold caring only for those inside, the church is a very partial church, if not a disobedient church. Can the church be the church in a world where at least three out of four people have yet to believe if it is not reaching out in agressive, effective evangelism?

But how is a growth conscience developed?

A church growth conscience is not built "in general" but in specifics into existing church structures. Each church, of course, is the Body of Christ, but it is also a set of officers, a board, committees, Christian women, youth, preaching, praying, music, and Christian education. Building a growth conscience means that the whole congregation, in all its structured parts, thinks in terms of effective evangelism. The structures of many churches are concerned exclusively with those who are already members. To build growth conscience means to build concern for those people "outside" into every organization of the church and denomination.

For example, Christian education must include both principles and practices of seeking non-Christians and gathering them into the fellowship. Nurture should increase Christians' knowledge of the Bible but also their knowledge of and experience in realistic, modern evangelism. Christian education should emphasize passages of Scripture that deal with carrying out God's unswerving purpose to save all people. The evangelistic thrust in the curriculum should begin at an early age and continue through adult classes. The curriculum should actively involve people in using their gifts and abilities to witness and evangelize. Congregations tend to get "walled off." Christian education should teach them how to climb over or tunnel under those walls. It should get members of all ages into evangelistic contact with their neighbors.

A growth conscience must not end in the local church. It must saturate both the denomination and the seminary. Most seminaries presently offer a course or two on evangelism, or perhaps even have a small department. Unfortunately, many offerings are electives and sterile, like describing a tennis game rather than teaching people how to play. The homiletics department is not much different. Most courses offered in that area teach students how to prepare sermons for existing churches. Do you know of a homiletics department which teaches students how to persuade hardcore pagans or preach effectively on the street or address skeptics and scoffers in a way that will win them? What a tremendous change might occur in America if all seminary classes were inflamed by evangelistic passion. Envision every professor in the seminary out planting new churches, or leading supporting congregations in Church Growth Seminars. This could revolutionize both seminaries and churches.

2. IDENTIFY NEEDS AND OPPORTUNITIES.

The time-honored business slogan "Find a need and fill it" has meaning for the church. In finding needs, one discovers opportunities; yet the church often misses opportunities because it is problem centered.

The church must focus on opportunities rather than problems. I recently conducted a series of seminars for one hundred churches of a denomination in the Midwest. Each church had a membership of a hundred or less. While working with them (many from rural communities), I made an interesting discovery. A major problem with small churches is that they think small. They are wrapped up in themselves. Their vision is limited, and they focus on their own problems. Typical small churches move from problem to problem. Their growth is stymied because they are so self-centered. For growth to occur in a little church, the congregation must break out of its problem syndrome and focus on opportunities.

However, many secondary needs exist. To structure need-assessment and opportunity-response into the ministry of a church, a mission committee or task force might be formed. Its purpose would be to search for and identify those needs and opportunities of the community to which the church could respond. This committee would gather facts and analyze data about the community. It would recommend programs for outreach, perhaps Bible study, evangelistic outreach, children's activities, or steps towards establishing a daughter church. Such a task force would give structure, form, purpose, and direction to evangelism and growth. Time should be given at every board and committee meeting to discussing opportunities for growth.

3. ESTABLISH FAITH GOALS.

There is spiritual power in a faith goal. A "leap of faith" develops dynamic spiritual power in an individual and in a congregation. To "risk" seems essential for growth. In growing churches willingness to "risk" is a common denominator. Such churches are willing to believe God for what they cannot see and to venture beyond their human resources. This is the basis of a faith goal, and it is the beginning of growth.

The Bible abounds with illustrations of people who have taken "leaps of faith." From Abraham, who "risked" by leaving his home for an unknown land, to Paul, who "risked" all, the inspired record illustrates again and again the power of faith. Such faith is pleasing to God, for "without faith it is impossible to please him" (Heb. 11:6).

One has little difficulty in mentally accepting and affirming the faith principle. It's the application that brings the rub. To let go of security is frightening. That security can be anything—an attitude, a possession, a habit, the status quo which freezes one into immobile inertia and blocks growth. The spiritual power of a faith goal can be the key which unlocks new doors of power and growth in the life of Christians and in the life of the church.

As a Church Growth consultant, I have seen how God uses the power of a faith goal. In seminars conducted by the Institute for American Church Growth, there is a time when a church, as a body of believers, exerts its combined faith in establishing a faith growth goal. This is usually a numerical goal. It is undergirded with the firm conviction that "numbers" are shorthand for "people." The goal is people who need to know Christ and who need to become disciples and responsible members of his church.

Near the conclusion of a Church Growth Seminar, the leaders of a small congregation had come to this moment of forming and projecting a faith goal. It was a rewarding experience to watch them struggle and achieve. At first they spoke as individuals: "*I* can do such and such." As the process continued, their speech evidenced a new relationship: "*We* can do this and this." They were beginning to speak as a body, as the Body of Christ. But the conversations changed again. From *I* to *we* to *he*! What would he, the head of the Body, desire for a faith goal? Listening to God is the first prerequisite for setting any goal. So a leap of faith was taken, a numerical goal was established. Following the seminar, this goal was structured into every board, department, and committee until it was "owned" by the entire congregation. At last report, this church was on target for its faith goal.

Is it scriptural to establish specific goals?

Scripture clearly supports such a concept. In the Gospels, we see how Jesus' life was goal directed. He said, "I must work the works of him that sent me" (John 9:4). Step by step, Jesus approached his goal—the cross. This goal was never far from him, for he had "come to seek and to save that which was lost" (Luke 19:10). Jesus' entire life was goal directed. The Apostle Paul was also goal directed. To the Philippians he wrote: "All I can say is this: forgetting what is behind me, and reaching out for that which lies ahead, I press towards the goal" (Phil. 3:13–14, NEB). Paul's burning desire was to be "all things to all men, that I might by all means save some" (1 Cor. 9:22, RSV). As a strategist for his Lord, Paul had specific plans and goals in planting new churches and winning people.

Does Scripture support numerical growth?

Yes! Numbers representing people are prominent in the growth of the early church as recorded in Acts. Luke could have referred to "a small group of believers," but he reported that "on a day when about 120 people were present" (Acts 1:15, LB). He could have spoken of "a large group who heard and believed on the day of Pentecost." Rather, Luke said, "Those who believed Peter were baptized—about 3,000 in all" (Acts 2:41, LB). Acts 4 speaks of the number of men who believed as about 5,000 (Acts 4:4). Specific numbers help us grasp the extent of God's blessing in the early church, even as specific goals today help focus our faith. Individuals and congregations who keep accurate accountings and establish specific goals do so upon solid biblical foundations.

Establishing a faith goal can be done only by each individual church, for each is as unique as a fingerprint. Based on its own vision, opportunities, resources, faith, and reason, a church projects a faith goal. Such a leap of faith is essential for both pastor and people even though they may not see how it will be accomplished. If God inspires a church to reach out, it must respond in faith.

A faith goal brushes aside nongrowth excuses. Nothing will ever be attempted if all objections must first be overcome. A faith goal is biblical, for Christ said, "I will build my church" (Matt. 16:18), and we become part of his master plan. A faith goal is an adventure with God, much as Abraham left Ur by faith for a strange land. Yet he journeyed, claiming God's promise, "I will make of thee a great nation, and I will bless thee, and make thy name great; and thou shalt be a blessing" (Gen. 12:2).

How big or how small should a faith goal be? That depends on you, your faith, and the faith of your church. Jesus spoke of faith to remove mountains. He also recognized that he could not do many mighty works because of their unbelief. The question is, What can we as a church believe God for? Scripture responds, "So be it according to your faith."

After establishing a faith goal for your church, the larger goal is then divided into smaller goals, each essential to accomplishing the overall task. Develop a "flow chart." Place the goal and the necessary enabling steps in some sequential order. Develop a time-line. Assign persons responsible. Devise methods and programs that promise to be most effective, and don't let fear of failure be a threat. If plans do not work, evaluate, recycle, and begin anew. Continue until you discover the formula that works best for your church. Monitor progress and results. Only with feedback can you determine progress toward achieving your objective. Accountability is important. Make your faith covenant with God, but share it with others who will help you toward your goal and will hold you accountable for its accomplishment.

A faith goal is not a tyrant but a target. It becomes that measurable objective, that central focus and goal of the church, which by faith is attainable.

4. INVOLVE LAYMEN AND TRAIN THEM.

If a church is serious about the Great Commission, the involvement of laity is of utmost importance. The growth of each church is uniquely dependent on its laity. The pastor who sees his or her role as an enabler to help laymen discover and utilize their unique gifts is far ahead of the pastor who tries to carry the whole load.

Laymen have many more gifts than are needed to maintain the existing body. Recognize and use gifts for outreach. This is an essential ingredient to a healthy, growing church. In *How to Grow a Church*, Donald McGavran responds to the question, Do you believe that in a congregation there are gifts for the growth of that church? He answers:

> You would misuse God's gifts if you used them solely for the service of existing Christians. As we see God's overwhelming concern for the salvation of men, we must assume that His gifts are given to men, at least in a part, that the lost may come to know Him, whom to know is life eternal.*

How do you go about involving laity?

All methods rest on the conviction that meaningful involvement on laity in outreach, according to their unique God-given gifts, is necessary for healthy church growth. Men, women, and youth must be helped to see the many ways in which they can

---

*Donald A. McGavran and Winfield C. Arn, *How to Grow a Church* (Glendale, CA: Regal Press, 1973).

evangelize. The concept of classes of leaders will go far toward getting Christians involved in evangelism. Here is a summation of the concept.

Class I Leaders—members whose energies are used primarily in the service of existing Christians.

Class II Leaders—members whose energies are primarily directed to serving and evangelizing non-Christians in their ministry area in an effort to bring them into the Body of Christ.

Class III Leaders—volunteer or partially paid leaders of evangelistic Bible study groups, new fellowships, chapels or small churches.

Class IV Leaders—full-time paid professional staff.

Class V Leaders—denominational or interdenominational leaders.

The key to dynamic, effective church growth is in recruiting, training, and utilizing Class II leaders.

A bar graph showing actual numbers of Class I and Class II leaders in the congregation helps many churches perceive that their energies, efforts, and finances are devoured in maintaining the church and that most of their leaders are Class I's. Recruiting Class II's then becomes reasonable and necessary.

Developing and structuring Class II leaders into the church program begins in the new members' class. These new believers are helped to discern the Body and to identify their gifts and abilities within the Body. Here they discover that all Christians are witnesses. They are taught to use their gifts in outreach ministry.

Structuring means training Class II leaders and providing various programs and opportunities for them. People involved in outreach ministry regularly meet together for encouragement and coordination, much as other boards and committees meet for their business.

Class II leaders should be recruited, trained, and deployed. They should be recognized and appreciated for their ministry. In a growing church, Class II leaders are the task force reaching those who have yet to believe.

5. RIGHTLY DISCERN "THE BODY."

There is no doubt the Body rightly understood, reverently discerned, and scientifically described assists Christian leaders in being better stewards of the grace of God and effective communicators of the gospel of Christ. As you will recall we emphasized in chapter 5 that the Body of Christ—the church—is a concrete entity made up of individual congregations and denominations. The more we know about the Body—its present condition, how it has grown—the more effective we will be in enabling that Body to reach its full potential in growth and outreach. Facts, totals and subtotals, and graphs and charts displaying data are needed to discern the Body. The data will tell much about the past, present, and future of each church. Research and information significantly enhances the possibility of projecting adequate strategies (review chap. 5 for more detail).

6. RIGHTLY DISCERN THE COMMUNITY.

A community is a mosaic of people. In chapter 6 we stressed that the more information and understanding a church can acquire about the people living all around it, the more effective it will be in evangelistic outreach. Discerning the community involves knowledge of population growth or decline, kinds of housing, age of housing, changes occurring in the community, and the ages, racial characteristics, ethnic distinctives, family structures, family incomes, employment characteristics, and educational backgrounds of the people. Secure the facts from the Chamber of Commerce, public library, schools, or the planning department of your state. The Census Bureau has abundant information available, broken down according to counties and cities.

As you try to make your evangelism more effective, compare the composition of church and community. The comparison will suggest many opportunities for evangelism. Fact gathering and interpretation of the community can be of great importance in developing effective strategy.

In most churches there are individuals whose professional occupations lend themselves to data gathering and display. A constant flow of community information, furnished perhaps by a small committee, should become a structural part of the congregation. Members in the church would then know the needs and opportunities in the community and could pray intelligently for an appropriate response.

7. DEVELOP EFFECTIVE STRATEGY.

An effective strategy is a strategy that works. It results in people receiving Christ and becoming part of his Body. An ineffective strategy does not produce growth. Ineffective strategies are to be analyzed and adjusted until they enable us to find the lost. If they cannot be made effective, discard them.

In developing effective strategies, remember that new units tend to be more productive than old units. A new convert has greater evangelistic potential than an old member. A new Sunday school class tends to be more effective in outreach than one which has been going for years. A large home Bible study, when divided, will tend to be twice as productive. A new church baptizes more people in proportion to its membership than an old congregation. Do not hesitate to look at groups which have existed for a long time and measure their productivity. If they prove to be ineffective, they should consider disbanding. If they are moderately effective, they should consider ways to become more effective. If they are effective, they should perhaps consider dividing to become twice as effective.

In Washington, D.C., the government is currently reviewing the innumerable boards and regulatory commissions and asking, "How many of these are necessary? How many really meet current needs?" Shouldn't there be a committee in every church continually looking through the light of accumulated data at the smaller activities and groups with respect to actual growth? Establish a system of accountability with a mandate from the board and pastor to determine whether or not a program is helping the church to reach out and grow. A constant review of the various activities of the church, from the sermon to the cradle roll, could be most productive. This technique is necessary. Business firms take inventory, look at their progress, eliminate unproductive areas, and recycle for greater effectiveness. The church can use this management technique to good advantage.

This would be very threatening for many churches.

The system of accountability works in business because the goal is clear—profit. In the church we are loath to establish clear, measurable goals; yet we must and then review our achievement in the light of them.

A second part of developing effective strategy is to be constantly seeking new, more effective methods. Study other churches to get concepts and ideas; then formulate plans and generate a constant flow of new input.

8. INVEST RESOURCES IN GROWTH.

By resources we mean time, talent, and treasure. A church's use of time correlates significantly with its pattern of growth. Lay leaders have only so much time to devote to the work of Christ and the church. Christians will, of course, witness on their jobs; yet for specific work after hours there is only so much consecrated time available. Lay leaders have jobs, homes, families, and other responsibilities. Hence, available time needs to be used wisely and well. A good beginning would be to measure the number of meetings and hours in a typical church month. The result would probably reveal that 90 percent or more of the available time turned inward and a small fraction turned outward toward non-Christians in the community.

If a church will devote the same number of hours and people to outreach that it devotes to its members, in one year that church will see significant growth.

Investing talent in outreach is a second important resource in structuring for growth. There is a tendency for congregations to put their best leaders and most talented members on boards and committees which turn inward toward maintaining the existing structure. The result is that the church may grow internally but fail to grow in membership.

In a large church in Pasadena, California, key leaders had been placed on boards and committees until all the significant members had been involved. One board had forty-five lay leaders. When these leaders saw how largely their time and talent focused inward, they came to a resounding conclusion—each board would be divided; half its members would be engaged in outreach, the other half in maintenance. A dramatic growth transformation has taken place in that church.

Finance is a third resource which must be wisely invested for growth. This is where structure really begins to pay off. If you want to know what a church is really concerned with, look at its budget. This shows where its real priorities lie. Any endeavor worthy of the name is reflected in the budget. Without financial backing, evangelism/Church Growth is not really part of the structure at either the congregational or denominational level.

Looking at your church budget, ask, "Does this represent where we really want our emphasis?" A large chruch with a budget of one hundred thousand dollars wasn't growing. It was designating only a few hundred dollars a year for evangelism. It had not structured evangelism into its organization, perhaps because it didn't have convictions or perhaps because it hadn't made them a part of the structure. But that was the chief reason it was not growing. Make sure that Church Growth thinking is reflected in your budget. Conviction should be backed up with dollars.

A study of growing churches indicates that approximately 10 percent or more of their gross budget is used to tell who they are, what they are, and where they are to people within their ministry area, and to tell them about Jesus in ways that really communicate. The budget is an excellent indicator of a church's priorities. Church Growth concerns are reflected in the budget. What are your church's real concerns?

9. GIVE PRIORITY TO EFFECTIVE EVANGELISM.

There are many kinds of evangelism—distributing tracts, meetings, bringing people to decisions. But an evangelism that counts itself imperfect or imcomplete until it brings people to Christ and into his church where they are integrated into the congregation is effective evangelism. It brings lost sons and daughters into the Father's house and makes them feel needed, wanted, and part of the inner structures of the church.

Some Christians say evangelism isn't really the function of the church. It is the function of the people. Christians living in the world will carry on evangelism.

In other words, some people say that evangelism is part of everything we do; therefore, we need give no attention to it. There is an element of truth to that, but a very small element! Until we consciously build evangelism into everything we do, until we are sure that evangelism is an essential part of every ministry of the church, not much evangelism will get done.

In structuring for evangelism, let us ask, Are we just sowing the field and allowing the weeds to take over? Are we sowing the field and allowing the wild animals to destroy it? Are we allowing the harvest to ripen and then fall and rot? Or, are we so proportioning our efforts that we sow, weed, and irrigate properly and reap so that the harvest ends up in the barn? This we must do! We must structure effective evangelism into every church program.

10. USE SPIRITUAL RESOURCES.

God's work should be done in God's way. Spiritual resources are an indispensable part of the mix—praying, witnessing, preaching, teaching, humble reliance on the Holy Spirit. These and other spiritual resources are available to the growing Christian and the growing church.

A common denominator of growing churches is fervent faith. This truth was first declared by John, writing from Patmos to the churches in Asia. To the church of Laodicea he wrote, "You are neither cold nor hot. . . . because you are . . . neither cold nor hot, I will spew you out of my mouth" (Rev. 3:15–16, RSV). A lukewarm church is nauseating. Speaking for the risen Christ, John was saying, "Stop being poor. Buy from me gold to make you truly rich. Stop being naked. Ask me for shining raiment. Give the Spirit his way in your life."

But how are spiritual resources structured into the church?

Let's illustrate through prayer. An organized, functioning prayer ministry is essential. The New Testament church practiced prayer; so must we.

A church might begin by teaching the value of prayer and underscoring the relationship between prayer and outreach. People would be challenged to pray for daughter churches, for conversions, for their Class II leaders, for new converts, and on and on. Volunteers would be enlisted for evangelism. Prayer-responsibility lists would be distributed and emphasize uncommitted families and individual prospects for salvation. Prayer chains might be formed. Keep records of the results of contacts and answered prayer, and encourage testimonies about answered prayer. Prayer for the "lost" can become an integral part of a church's ministry.

Structuring spiritual resources into the growth of the church may be the most important thing we have yet said. Structuring must not come to members as a new load. Can you hear Christians saying, "Oh, how I have to do all this additional work." That would be self-defeating. Spiritual resources are structured in so Christians will feel a great joy, a great surge of power, sweeping through them. Then they will feel part of the work of the Holy Spirit! When correctly built in, spiritual resources will make Christians feel they would rather be doing God's will than anything else.

QUESTIONS FOR REVIEW AND DISCUSSION

1. Evaluate your church's ministry in each of the ten areas.
2. How could each of the ten steps listed be built into your own particular church?
3. Discuss a faith goal and set one for your church.
4. Develop a graph depicting the Class I and Class II leaders in your church.

5. Complete the worksheets in Appendix B. Study and discuss these findings as they relate to your church's future growth.
6. What is your church's present strategy for growth? What areas could be pruned? What could be emphasized?
7. Make a graph of the budget allocations of the church. Where does this indicate priorities lie?
8. Are the evangelism efforts of your church effective? Make a list of things being done and evaluate them in terms of their effectiveness.
9. How can you direct the spiritual gifts and resources of your church toward growth and outreach?

10

Churches Grow As They Risk for Growth

You've talked about the Great Commission. Can it really be fulfilled?

The history of the church is the miracle of ordinary Christians who had one thing in common—faith in God! Walking by faith, they believed God's promises to be completely trustworthy, no matter what the circumstances. Seeing the possibilities, they dared try the seemingly impossible.

The greatest proof that the impossible is possible is the empty tomb. Jesus Christ is alive! And that fact is the most effective means of dealing with those who say, "It can't be done!" The first Christians were, for the most part, poor and uneducated but obedient to their Lord. They grew from 120 to 3000 to 5000. By faith the church moved out, empowered by the Holy Spirit. As Luke recorded, they turned their world upside down.

Faith is venturing out to do what God wants done, even if nobody believes it can be done. The test of faith is whether one really ventures his life and soul on things hoped for. Does the vision compel the pilgrimage? Does the pilgrimage go forward in spite of dangers, obstacles, and "lions in the way?"

In spite of opposition and severe difficulties, men and women of faith have ventured forth to spread the Good News. One hundred years after David Livingstone, Africa, south of the Sahara, is in the process of becoming substantially Christian. By faith, men and women are accomplishing the impossible, surmounting insurmountable difficulties.

The Great Commission flies over the church like a banner. Can it be fulfilled? Of course! The Lord will give us strength and power to fulfill it. Indeed, the Great Commission applies to every band of Christians, every church, every denomination. All are commissioned to make disciples. We must continually go forward until the three billion who have yet to believe, have believed, or at least have really heard the Good News.

I'm not sure everyone in my church believes it's possible.

There have always been doubters and scoffers. Scripture records that even Thomas, the apostle, refused to believe until he could see and touch the prints of the nails, the wound, in Jesus' side. How many early Christians saw the possibilities in Saul of Tarsus as he persecuted the church? How many could see him as Paul, the missionary, the strategist, the apostle? The early church was not filled with "super saints"; they had their doubters and scoffers as well. Yet faith overcame!

Venturing in faith is foundational for spreading the Gospel. In spite of physical dangers, David Livingstone ventured forth to take Jesus Christ to the savage, unreached people of Africa. William Carey left his livelihood as a shoemaker to take Christ to India. Many tried to discourage him, but he was obedient to God's command and opened a continent to the gospel. Robert Morrison sailed to China in face of numerous "reasons" that it couldn't be done. These men had faith to believe that it could, should, and would be done and that God had called them to do it!

Thousands upon thousands of illustrations throughout the history of the church show that faith overcame doubt. While the task may seem impossible to the individual Christian or to the individual church, remember, many commands and promises of

Scripture are given not only to *you* but to the Body of Christ. *I* can't do it, *you* can't do it; but, empowered by the Holy Spirit, *we*, the church, can do it.

You're saying that expectant faith is of primary importance?

Unquestionably! A major problem facing thousands of churches across America is a low level of faith in their ability to reach out and grow. This mental block poses a serious threat to any and all possibilities. Unless faith is increased, little serious effort will accompany plans for growth; yet most churches have the potential for far greater effectiveness than their present level of achievement.

In our Church Growth Seminars and training sessions, "seeing the possibilities" is an important first step. It enables pastors and lay leaders to see and believe that God desires his Church to grow, that growth is possible for their churches in their unique environment. This foundation stone makes it possible to consider new plans and possibilities. "I now realize we can grow." "You have helped us discover new horizons and find new possibilities." "It's *possible*! God will direct our efforts." "I see my gifts and the growth of my church in an exciting new way." These are typical comments written by lay leaders on evaluation sheets at the conclusion of a seminar. Such faith opens doors for outreach and effective ministry.

Expectations, in reality, are faith in action, faith that results in dynamic, living churches. The biblical mandate for making disciples demands that nonproductive attitudes which keep performance expectations at low levels be changed.

The First Baptist Church of Houston, Texas, has experienced significant growth. During his first year, Pastor Bisagno saw over one thousand members added, along with twelve new staff. Yet he relates that during the early months of this pastorate, something was missing, and he was unable to identify it.

Pastor Bisagno described his discovery of the missing element in *How to Build an Evangelistic Church.*

One Sunday morning, fifty-one people received Christ. The following Sunday it happened! That intangible something I had missed was there. I did not know what it was I was looking for until I reviewed that service again and again. The thing that made the difference, expectancy—an air of excitement, hope, vision—expectancy was in the air. It is there every Sunday now. I realistically know, and you know, that we will probably never win everyone in Houston to Christ, but I don't want anyone telling my people that. They are almost convinced that they can! They are expecting to do it! They are expecting packed audiences, souls saved, lives changed, fire from heaven every Sunday.*

This expectancy—belief that God is actively involved in the life and outreach of the congregation—provides the foundation for growth and ministry of the church. It should be foundational in the life of every church.

The power of expectancy can be seen in two churches only a few blocks apart. One has stopped growing and begun to decline. The other evidences vigorous growth and vitality. What accounts for the difference? The difference is not in the building, for they are the same basic plants. Nor is it in the preaching. The significant difference is that in one church people expect something to happen; they expect God to move, and their faith is met. Which do you imagine is the growing church?

Faith then is the key for the growth of my church?

Yes, faith and *works*! Churches do not grow just being there, by carrying on good worship services, by vague good deeds, or by looking after existing Christians. Churches grow by putting into effect decisive bold plans which intend Church Growth and which have been bathed in prayer, vision, faith, and obedience.

The importance of obedience can be seen in the transformation

---

*John R. Bisagno, *How to Build an Evangelistic Church* (Nashville: Broadman Press, 1971).

of a local church in Ohio. People asked what had happened. Was it a miracle, a revival, or a revolution?

It was all three; yet it was none of them. For years the church had struggled along, increasing here, decreasing there, never experiencing real growth or vitality. Then the breakthrough! It involved the same people and the same pastor, but something happened.

Pastor and people began to perceive themselves and their tasks in new ways. Previously, their performance as Christians could have been classified as "average." Members functioned as expected; they came, sang, prayed, listened, and left. But with the breakthrough, "average" changed to "excellent," and the church began to experience exciting growth and vitality.

How was this new excellence achieved? There were no major changes in leadership, no reorganization, no new programs, no new locations. The key to the turnaround was a thought-through, prayed-through, God-inspired decision made by pastor and key lay leaders: The church can and must make significant gains in implementing the biblical commission to make disciples.

Obedience began with decision. That was the focal point. Later many programs were implemented in translating determination into measurable results, but these programs would have been entirely ineffective without a clear mandate to redirect the church's energies to be more effective stewards of the entrusted riches of Christ.

Church Growth is obedience to God, not a program or lines on a graph or any new methodology or passing fad. Church Growth is obedience to the command of the one who said, "Go and make disciples!"

People who draw up bold plans measure effectiveness by how many people are, in fact, added to the Lord and how many new congregations are brought into existence.

One mark of the Church Growth school of thought is pragmatism in regard to methods but not in regard to truth. Truth is truth whether anybody believes it or not. The atonement of the

Lord Jesus was just as true when he was dying alone on the cross, without any believers, as it was when Whitfield, Moody, Wesley, and others were bringing multitudes to confess him and to become his disciples.

Pragmatism as to method is a different thing. If our activities are leading men and women to Christ, making them responsible members of his church, and adding new congregations to the Body, then we continue. If what we are doing does not produce these results, then we must either modify or discard our behavior for activity that does. God desires the Gospel proclaimed to the ends of the earth and commands us to make disciples of all men. This same God blesses to the growth of his church businesslike, effective plans drawn up by his servants who intend to obey him, to disciple multitudes of men and women, and to plant new churches.

Faith, works, expectations, plans, obedience—but is there more?

Yes! New life and growth are more likely to be experienced when a church (or individual Christian) is willing to *risk* and move from the known to the unknown. Such a move, however, is threatening. Raising expectation levels is threatening. Not all clergymen and congregations are willing to assume risk. During a recent Church Growth Conference for a local congregation, those in attendance agreed it would be pleasing to God and a step of faith and obedience to double their membership in the next five years. The pastor, while agreeing with this goal, wanted no part of the newly formed "task force for growth." He chose a stance some distance removed from the project. He later confided, "Suppose the goal proves too ambitious and is not reached? Think of my embarrassment if I am a part." He was not prepared to risk.

Such fear of failure has laid to rest many attainable goals and buried many magnificent visions. Fear comes to the fore in such attitudes as "Will not greater demand increase the resistance from members?" or "Will I, as the leader, be rejected for not meeting these high goals?" For a pastor or a church to allow fear of failure to determine the future is the greatest of all failures. Better the ancient admonition of Herodotus: "It is better by noble boldness to risk being subject to half the evils we anticipate than to remain in cowardly listlessness for fear of what may happen."

To minimize the risk of high expectations, many nongrowth excuses are conceived. The rationalizing approach says, "People in this church already know what the goals are. If they don't like them, they can go elsewhere." A nongrowth person says, "We are going at full speed now." This gives the illusion that the church is operating at the outer limits when, in fact, it is far from it. A third dodge is using the "program approach." Leaders hope that better results will be achieved by introducing more and hopefully better new programs. "This new program will solve our attendance problems. After all, look what it did for that church."

Still other neutralizers use the "carrot approach" which promises rewards for performance. "Bring three new people this Sunday, and you will win a . . ." All these approaches skirt the real issue: Do we have the basic biblical and theological conviction that we *can* and *must* achieve better results if we are to be faithful to Christ's command to make disciples?

Such a commitment for growth is verbalized by Pastor Tom Wolf in the film *They Said It Couldn't Be Done*. Taking a church that the denomination planned to close, Tom Wolf was willing to risk.

> Our church, when I first came, was facing a situation which many congregations face. At one time, the church had been a fairly good size . . . it had been prospering. Then the community began to change and the church began to go down. There were internal problems . . . there were fear without, conflicts within. There were rapid pastoral changes. The congregation was not really growing and reaching the community; but I knew that God had brought this congregation to a place where they were very desperate. At the time there had been discussion of selling the building and moving to a different place. If I had not believed that God was going to do a work, I'll be honest with you, I would have given up a long time ago.

I remember when we first saw the church. Afterward, I remember going up on a monument near here. As I saw the city spread out around me, I said, "Lord, give us this area. Whatever you have to do . . . if you have to break me . . . I pray, God, give this place to your people and bring glory to Jesus Christ."

Since we have been here, we have grown each year eighteen to twenty percent. We have seen our mission budget grow, but our concentration has been, "Lord use me here." God has promised me, through His Word, that if I will do His work in His way, He will bring victory. I am confident that what God is doing here is in anticipation of what He is going to do in the future. He has overcome obstacles . . . and every obstacle that He overcomes right now is God's guarantee that He can do it again . . . and He will do it again!

Will this work for me?

Perhaps a way to answer your question is with an illustration from Dr. Arn's experience.

"Jump . . . go ahead . . . jump!" The words flew upward from boys and girls some sixty feet below. High above, I clutched the bar of a trapeze swinging back and forth in great arcs. At the apex of each swing, an empty trapeze bar came temptingly close. "Jump . . . go ahead . . . jump!"

How did I get in such a predicament? A fine group of talented teens had formed a youth circus. They presented a varied and unique program of tumbling, juggling, and trampoline, all with humor, costumes, and equipment. The suspense-filled climax to the performance was the high trapeze act where performers flipped, twirled, and twisted in an aerial extravaganza which brought gasps from the audience and thunderous applause.

This talented group formed the cast for a film I was producing entitled *Circus*. One afternoon while waiting for the photographer, one youth turned to me, pointed to the high trapeze, and said, "Why don't you try it?" I quickly changed the conversation, but other youths heard the challenge and joined the growing chorus. "Try it . . . try it!" Eyeing the large safety net under the paraphernalia, I cautiously replied, "Well . . . why not!"

Very slowly and very carefully I began to climb the small rope ladder. Twenty feet . . . thirty feet . . . thirty-five . . . forty thousand . . . fifty thousand . . . finally I crawled onto a minuscule platform which seemed miles above the assembled crowd. I looked down. The once large safety net had shrunk to unbelievably small proportions. A slight breeze caused the platform to sway and the wires softly sigh.

"Go ahead, you can do it!" the youths encouraged. Taking the trapeze bar in my perspiring hands and steadying my shaking knees, I prepared to jump. Across from my platform a youth was ready to send forth the empty trapeze. Mustering up all my courage, I cried, "Go!" and went swinging into space.

Flying through the air, I made three important discoveries. First, you can't hold on to one bar while grasping for the other. You must let both hands go and leap! Second, it's frightening and threatening to let go of your security. Third, you don't have forever to make up your mind.

"Jump . . go ahead . . . jump!" On the third arc I did! Flying through the air, I reached out and grasped the bar with my fingertips, went swinging to the other side, and was pulled safely to the platform. Amid the applause and cheers of the youths below, I had taken a leap of faith.

Faith, to me, is that confident assurance that sets us free to try the impossible and is brought about as we are willing to take the leap. It is not enough just to know about faith. Each church has to climb up to its own trapeze, step by step. The higher you climb, the harder it will seem. When the top is reached and you are ready for your leap of faith, you will ask, "Will it work for me?" There's one way to find out. Try it! . . . go ahead . . . try it!

QUESTIONS FOR REVIEW AND DISCUSSION

1. Discuss leaps of faith you have taken and results.
2. What possibilities can you see for your church in five years? Write down your expectations for your church five years from now.

3. Is there a sense of expectancy in your church? Why or why not? What would increase that sense of expectancy?
4. What would a pragmatic look at your church include? What new insights did you find in doing this?
5. What could be your church's next leap of faith?
6. Make a list of steps your church should take for growth.

Glossary

Biblical Principles—truths revealed in Scripture, founded on revelation, and believed as bedrock to the faith.

Church Growth—an application of biblical, theological, anthropological, and sociological principles to congregations and denominations and to their communities in an effort to disciple the greatest number of people for Jesus Christ. Believing that "it is God's will that His Church grow and His lost children be found," Church Growth endeavors to devise strategies, develop objectives, and apply proven principles of growth to individual congregations, to denominations, and to the worldwide Body of Christ.

Church Growth Conscience—the conviction that God's will is for the Body of Christ to grow.

Church Growth Eyes—a characteristic of Christians who have achieved an ability to see the possibilities for growth and to apply appropriate strategies to gain maximum results for Christ and His Church.

Church Growth Principle—a worldwide truth which, when properly applied, along with other principles, contributes significantly to the growth of the church.

Church Growth, Types of:
   1. *Internal*—growth of Christians in grace, relationship to God, and to one another.
   2. *Expansion*—growth of the church by the evangelization of non-Christians within its ministry area.
   3. *Extension*—growth of the church by the establishment of daugh-

ter churches within the same general homogeneous group and geographical area.

4. *Bridging*—growth of the church by establishing churches in significantly different cultural and geographical areas.

Church Growth, Ways of Increase:

1. *Biological growth*—children of existing members who come into the church.

2. *Transfer growth*—members of one church who unite with another church.

3. *Conversion growth*—the coming into the church of people of the world who are converted by receiving Jesus Christ as Lord and Savior.

Church Growth, Ways of Decrease:

1. *Death*—members of a church called home to be with the Lord.

2. *Transfer*—members of a church who leave and unite with another church.

3. *Reversion*—members of the church who renounce Christian faith and are no longer part of the community of faith.

Classes of Leadership:

Class 1—leaders whose energies primarily turn inward toward the service of existing Christians and existing church structures.

Class 2—leaders whose energies primarily turn outward toward non-Christians in an effort to bring them into the Body of Christ.

Class 3—leaders who are unpaid or partially paid and who shepherd new small churches.

Class 4—leaders who are full-time, paid professional staff of on-going churches.

Class 5—denominational or interdenominational leaders.

Decision—a personal commitment to receive Jesus Christ as Savior.

Discerning the Body—seeing a local church or a denomination as it really is and obtaining and analyzing information about it and its members.

Discerning the Community—seeing a church's ministry area in its sociological, economic, and ethnic composition and obtaining and analyzing information about it.

Disciple (noun)—a person who has made a commitment to Jesus Christ as Lord and Savior, who is learning and practicing His teachings, and who maintains a meaningful relationship with His Body—the Church—and its mission of spreading the Gospel.

Disciple (verb)—to bring a person to faith in Christ and obedient membership in His Church.

Evangelism, Classifications:

Evangelism Zero (E-0)—winning nominal Christians back to fervent faith.

Evangelism One (E-1)—evangelization of non-Christians in one's own language and culture.

Evangelism Two (E-2)—evangelization of non-Christians in a similar language and culture.

Evangelism Three (E-3)—evangelization of non-Christians of a radically different language and culture.

Great Commission Goal—a cell (church) of committed Christians in every thousand of the earth's population, that is, in every part of every city and in every country throughout the world, a group in which people can hear the Gospel from and see it demonstrated by their own intimates in their own tongue and thus have a reasonable opportunity to become disciples of Jesus Christ.

Homogeneous Group—a group of people who all have some characteristic in common and feel that they "belong."

Measuring Growth—using diagnostic instruments to determine the growth/decline of a church.

Ministry Area—that area within a reasonable driving distance of a church.

Mix—that combination of ingredients which taken together and in the right proportions produces effective church growth.

Mosaic—the variety of cultural, ethnic, economic, educational, and linguistic groupings of people found in a city, country, state, or nation.

New Testament Church—a church which intends to be like the churches described in the New Testament, especially in regard to the propagation of the Gospel, in other words, a church concerned with, engaged in, and successful at establishing new congregations.

Nongrowth Excuses—rationalizations of failure to grow, often used as justification for nongrowth.

Receptivity—openness to hear, consider, and obey the Gospel of Jesus Christ. Individuals, groups, and societies show varying degrees of receptivity.

Removing the Fog—the process of penetrating the rationalizations, propaganda, inaccuracies, and unknowns and getting at the facts concerning the growth history, present condition, and future possibilities of churches and denominations.

Responsive Area—a section of a city or countryside from which individuals and groups do become Christians.

Risk—daring to attempt the seemingly impossible.

Scientific Method—measuring exactly and in such a way that other investigators using the same measuring devices will obtain the same results; in short, looking at the church with the same common sense and good judgment that we use in other areas of life.

Structuring for Growth—mobilizing members, organizations, and activities in a local church or a denomination toward a common goal of growth.

Appendix A: Church Growth Films, Cassettes, Posters, and Magazine

The items listed below are available from Christian Communication, 150 South Los Robles Ave., Pasadena, California 91101; (213) 449-4400. A catalog of other Church Growth resources is also available from the same address.

FILMS

Reach Out and Grow—28 min., color, 16 mm
> A film to inspire, motivate, and challenge church members to meaningful commitment and involvement in their church and to help viewers discover the necessity of discipleship and how their gifts are essential for growth and outreach.
> Rental: $25.00

How to Grow a Church—26 min., color, 16 mm
> The message of this film is that it is God's will for his church to grow and for his lost children to be found. It is effective in encouraging growing churches to continue or increase their growth, in encouraging plateau churches to find new life and growth, and in encouraging declining churches to make bold new plans for growth.
> Rental: $25.00

Planned Parenthood for Churches—20 min., color, 16 mm
This dramatic film tells the story of a church that discovered the need and opportunity to establish a new congregation. Church growth principles are communicated with warmth and humor. Viewers will be sensitized to opportunities and possibilities for extension growth.
Rental: $25.00

. . . *And They Said It Couldn't Be Done!*—28 min., color, 16 mm
This film applies faith to three areas: realizing the Great Commission; possibilities in and through the local church; and confident assurance, by faith, in overcoming personal obstacles.
Rental: $30.00

Exploring the Churches of the Revelation—a series of 8 films, each approximately 5 min. in length.
Patmos, Ephesus, Smyrna, Pergamum, Thyatira, Sardis, Philadelphia, Laodicea. The strengths and weaknesses of the Revelation churches provide illuminating insights for the growth of the church today.
First film free when ordering the series ($8.00 each).

Building the Church—a series of 6 films, each 5 min. in length.
The Apostle Paul, Paul in Philippi, Paul in Thessalonica, Paul in Corinth, Paul in Ephesus, Paul in Rome. A resource to help examine the basic strategy the Apostle Paul employed in living the Christian life and in building the early church.
First film free when ordering the entire series ($8.00 each).

Solo—15 min., color, 16 mm
A thrilling hymn to the challenge of mountain climbing which has a unique correlary to church growth.
Rental: $16.50

All rental prices are plus film damage insurance and shipping costs.

CASSETTES:

Two 28-minute sessions on Church Growth which include principles, questions and answers, personal experiences, and new growth ideas/concepts. Taken from the films *How to Grow a Church* and *Reach Out and Grow*.

POSTERS:

Six colorful posters 11 × 34 to delightfully keep Church Growth in front of lay people. They fit well on any bulletin board or wall in the church. Directly and indirectly they say to all who see them, "Let's grow and make disciples!" Set of 6—$8.50, plus postage.

MAGAZINE:

Church Growth: America is a bi-monthly magazine of information, instruction, and inspiration. The first step for a church—the pastor and people—is to see the possibilities. *Church Growth: America* is a unique and distinctive resource. It contains new growth ideas and concepts, research data, principles of growth, help in formulating strategies and bold plans, solutions to growth-restricting problems and new growth of your church. It is an effective communicative bulletin and can be utilized by pastors, official boards, evangelism committees, and others concerned with growth and evangelism. A year's subscription is $8.50 and may be obtained at the following address: Christian Communication, 150 South Los Robles Ave., Pasadena, California 91101.

Appendix B: Your Church

YOUR CHURCH STATISTICALLY

Statistics provide a type of shorthand, and numbers become symbols to help us think constructively and skillfully about people and the church.

This section will help you understand your church better when you complete it as accurately as possible.

A. *Overall Membership Statistics*

Year	Church Membership	Attendance AM Service	Sunday Sch. Enrollment	Sunday Sch. Attendance

(Use dates for the past 10 years)

B. *Church Membership by Age Groups*

Age	Number	Percentage*
10–14		
15–19		
20–24		
25–29		
30–34		
35–39		
40–44		
45–49		
50–54		
55–59		
60–64		
65–69		
70–74		
75 +		
Total		

*To find percentage: divide the number of members in the age group by the total membership.

Example: total $\overline{)\text{members in age group}}^{\text{percentage}}$

$180 \overline{)36.00}^{.20}$ or 20%

C. Membership Flow

1. How your church grows is important. A church grows in three ways: *conversion growth*—when people receive Christ and become part of the fellowship; *transfer growth*—when people enter into membership by letter of transfer; *biological growth*—when children of members also become members after their profession of faith.

   During the last 12 months, how did your church grow?

   Members were added to our church in the following ways:

	Number	% of Total New Members
Conversion		
Transfer-in		
Biological		

2. It is also important to know how people are separated from the church.

   Members were separated from our church in the following ways:

	Number	% of Total Members Separated
Re-version		
Transfer-out		
Death		

D. *Participation*

1. Of the total membership, what number are involved in some form of service (deacon, teacher, committee, etc.)?

   Total membership _____

   Number involved _____

2. Those involved in some forms of service may be classified as Class I or Class II workers. Class I is defined as those individuals whose energies serve the existing church, that is, their energies are turned inward. Class II workers are those individuals whose energies are turned outward, that is, toward reaching those in the community for Jesus Christ.

   Of the number of individuals involved in service, classify them according to the following:

   Number of Class I workers _____
   Number of Class II workers _____

Family Units

1. Think in terms of complete family units for a moment (all of a family living under one roof), and look at the total number of people participating in the church, then the number of individuals whose families are not involved as family units.

   We have _____ family units participating as families.

   We have _____ individuals whose families are not involved.

"Grow where you are planted" is a good assertion, but where are you planted? Take a closer look at the community; in so doing, the church could find a more effective ministry to the community and its people.

A. Secure a map of your community.
   1. Place a black dot on the map for each member, according to his residence (one dot per family).
   2. Can you generally identify any homogenous groups on this map (income, education, race, etc.)?
   3. Place a red dot on the map for every church within a 3-mile radius of your church.
B. Secure from the Chamber of Commerce growth figures of your community over the past 10 years and the growth projection for the next 10 years.
   1. Record these figures:

MY COMMUNITY

	Year	Population		Year	Projection
(Use dates for last 10 years)			*(Use dates for next 10 years)*		